Vocalizing With Ease:

a Self-Improvement Guide

Carmen Lancaster
463-8854

Linda Rammage, PhD

illustrations: ***Michiel Haijtink***

ACKNOWLEDGEMENTS:

I wish to thank Anne Gardner for her helpful suggestions and advice. Thanks to Murray Morrison and Scott Durham for their help with editing. Sincere appreciation to my novice-trial editors: Christine Ghose, Shanti Ghose, Robin Kimpton and Jean Rammage. Thanks also to my Mom and Dad for their financial support. I extend my gratitude to all my colleagues from many different disciplines who have influenced my therapy style; and a special word of thanks goes to many patients and clients who have helped me discover and confirm reliable techniques for voice improvement, and provided encouragement and inspiration throughout the years.

Thanks to the folks at Broadway Printers for their expert work and patience.

Finally, Thank-you, Michiel, for offering your artistic talent and keen sense of humour to make this self-help program fun!

National Library of Canada
ISBN 0-9680436-0-7

Direct any inquiries to:
Linda Rammage
The Voice Clinic, 805 West 12th Ave, Vancouver, B.C., V5Z 1M9

TABLE OF CONTENTS

DEDICATION:

This book is dedicated to the memory of my dear friends ***Danna Koschkee*** *and* ***Brian Smith,*** *who devoted their lives to helping people with communication challenges.*

Brian *and* ***Danna*** *brought hope and happiness to everyone who had the good fortune to know and love them. They inspired and empowered their clients, students and colleagues ...*

I hope the information in this book will inspire and empower you and your voice!

Linda

Vocalizing With Ease: A Self-Improvement Guide

by: ***Linda Rammage***

INTRODUCTION:

There is always room for improvement in physical function, including use of our voices. Since speech and voice are windows to the soul, voice enhancement requires an appreciation of the link between thoughts, emotions and movement. In order to improve the act of speaking, we need to be aware of our emotional reactions, physical responses and vocal habits.

This is a therapy guide book for people who want to improve their voices. It will be helpful to individuals who are experiencing voice problems due to improper muscle use, and for people, from all walks and talks of life, who wish to prevent voice problems. The information and exercises are suitable for adults and children who are motivated to work toward improving their speech and voice skills. If you are experiencing problems with your voice, a qualified voice therapist can guide you, so you benefit most from the information in this book.

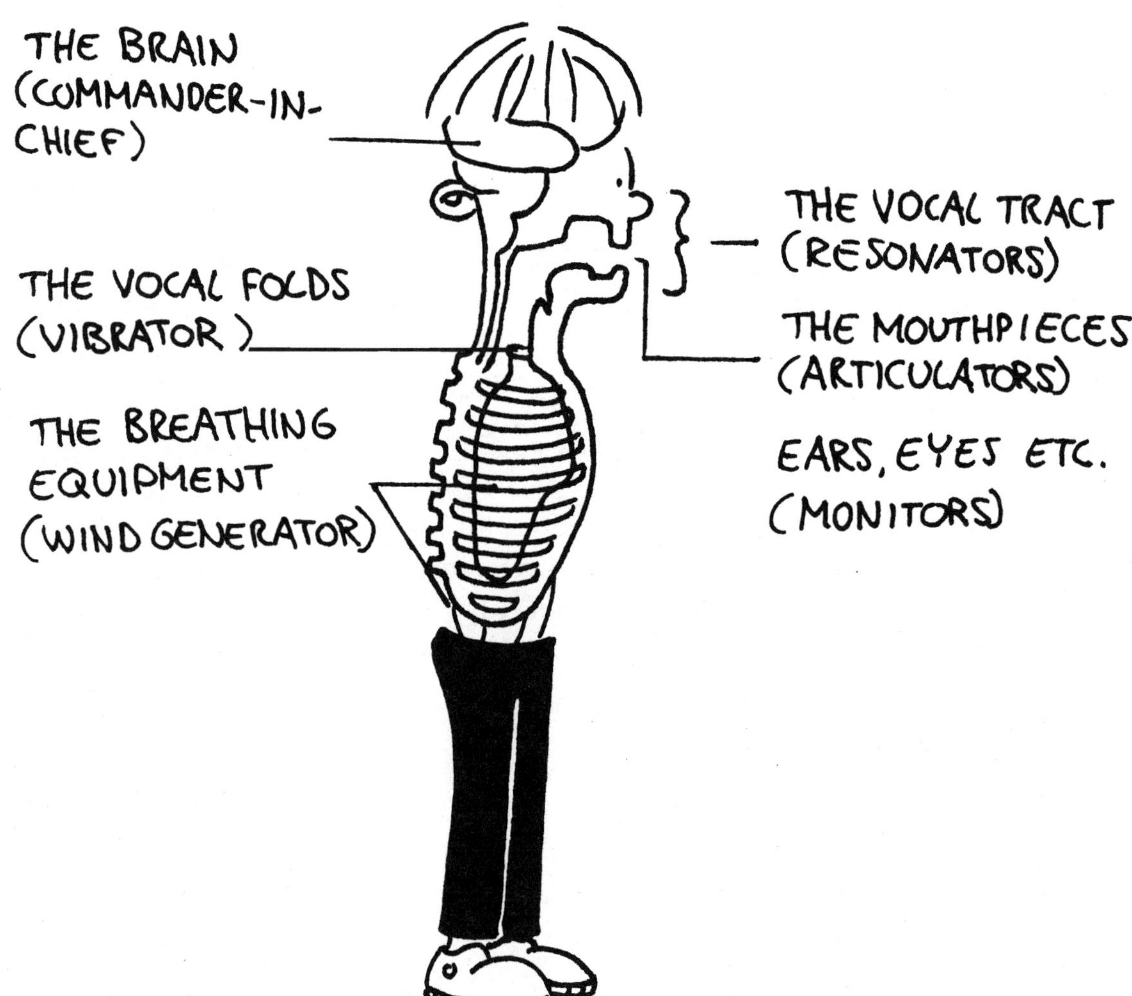

HUMAN SPEECH MODEL

SECTION 1:

What Voice Is, and How Your Speech Equipment Works

We usually refer to voice production in the context of speaking or singing. Vocalizing is simply one component of the human behaviour we call "speech". Of course, you can vocalize without communicating anything at all, for example, when you say (or sing) "aaaaah..." on a single note without intending to convey any particular message.

The vocalizing activity most of us use most often is the one we call "talking": when your voice and speech equipment work together to send a message out-loud to another person (or your dog, cat, computer ... or even yourself).

We often think of the voice equipment as living in the "voicebox" in the neck (known in medical books as the larynx). The speech equipment includes many other body parts as well. The easiest way to begin understanding how it works is to describe the main jobs of the different body parts used when we vocalize and talk.

Body Part #1:

The Commander-In-Chief: The Brain

THE BRAIN is the commander of the speech and voice equipment. It works something like a very sophisticated computer by creating and organizing ideas, turning them into language, then sending electrical-type signals through nerves to muscles that will contract and relax to make speech movements.

During speech, millions of brain cells send millions of impulses to many groups of muscles in just the right sequence so all the speech equipment will work properly. The brain also integrates information from the ears and other body monitors as we talk and listen, and adjusts our speech program based on this input.

Because the brain is the chief organizer and decision-maker for all body actions, it has a lot of power over the final speech product...

> For example, if the brain senses that we're in a big hurry, it may force us to work our speech and voice muscles very quickly and tensely ... When this happens, we may feel like our mouth is getting ahead of our brain: we stumble on our words, run out of breath, lose track of what we are saying, and end up repeating ourselves. If the brain notices competing noise it may command us to force the voice out louder than is comfortable, by squeezing muscles in the throat.

Since the brain takes our emotions and general goals into account when it's planning the speech movements, it may do some "editing" of our intended message...

> For example, if the brain decides that what we are thinking or feeling may get us into big trouble, it may command the muscles to say the words in a very quiet voice, so the message won't seem so "bad". In some cases, it may squeeze the muscles in the voice equipment very tight, so the incriminating words don't come out at all.

Body Part #2:

The Wind Generator: The Breathing Machine

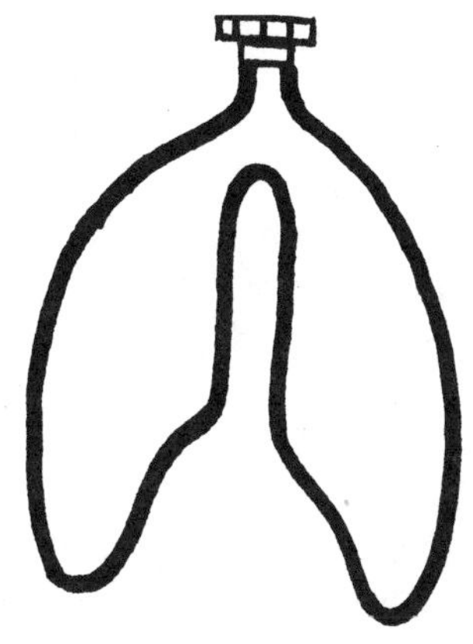

The way we use the breathing machine during speech is very complicated. Luckily, like most complicated actions such as walking and eating, breathing to communicate is an automatic function we're born with. After all, babies don't have to think twice about how to use their breath to vocalize in a way that gets our attention very quickly!

The lungs are our fuel tanks for speech. The fuel, of course, is air. When the brain commands the breathing system to start the speech operation, muscles and elastic tissue compress the air in the lungs. Because the air is compressed or "squeezed", it flows out of the lungs through the windpipe on its way toward the vocal folds. This outward flow of air from the lungs is the raw power for voice production. The amount and speed of airflow contribute to the power, pitch and quality of the vocal tone. We will study in more detail how the airflow contributes to speech sound production in the next section. For now, you can gain a sense of how the breathing and voice equipment work together if you conduct a little experiment:

Think for a minute of something you've learned recently that surprised or interested you: some piece of juicy gossip, or something you may have learned in the last few paragraphs; if you react to this new information tidbit vocally, you will make a sudden and brief vocal sound like:

"hm!" *(an abbreviation for: "Say, that's interesting!")*

Try responding to your thoughts several times in this way:

"hm!" ... "hm!" ... "hm!" ... *(Don't think about how you're producing this sound, just notice* ***what it feels like....)***

Allow me to guide you as you explore what you feel:

During "hm!" do you feel the abdominal muscles working?
(correct answer: "yes")

If you repeat the "hm!" response several times, do you feel a corresponding number of abdominal muscle actions?
(correct answer: "yes")

Do you happen to feel a release or "relaxation" of the abdominal muscles following each "hm!" response?
(correct answer: "yes")

Do you need to take a big breath before you can say "hm!"?
(correct answer: "no, the lungs always have air in them")

Like any system run by fuel, the vocal fuel supply needs to be replenished regularly. As you discovered during your experiment, breathing in to replenish the air supply occurs automatically when you stop squeezing the lung-compressing muscles: then the lower torso can relax to let the diaphragm do its work of breathing in. You might want to become familiar with some of the breathing parts, by exploring their locations and actions...

The diaphragm is the main muscle that lets us breathe in. It works with the ribcage-lifting muscles to expand the lung cavity. You can identify the location of your diaphragm by feeling your bottom rib, and tracing it all the way around your body. The diaphragm is a large sheet of muscle attached to the bottom rib; it divides your torso into two sections: the upper section houses the lungs and heart; the lower section is where all the other "guts" live. In its rest position, the diaphragm is dome-shaped. When it works to help us breathe in, the diaphragm flattens against the guts in the lower torso, expanding the lung cavity vertically.

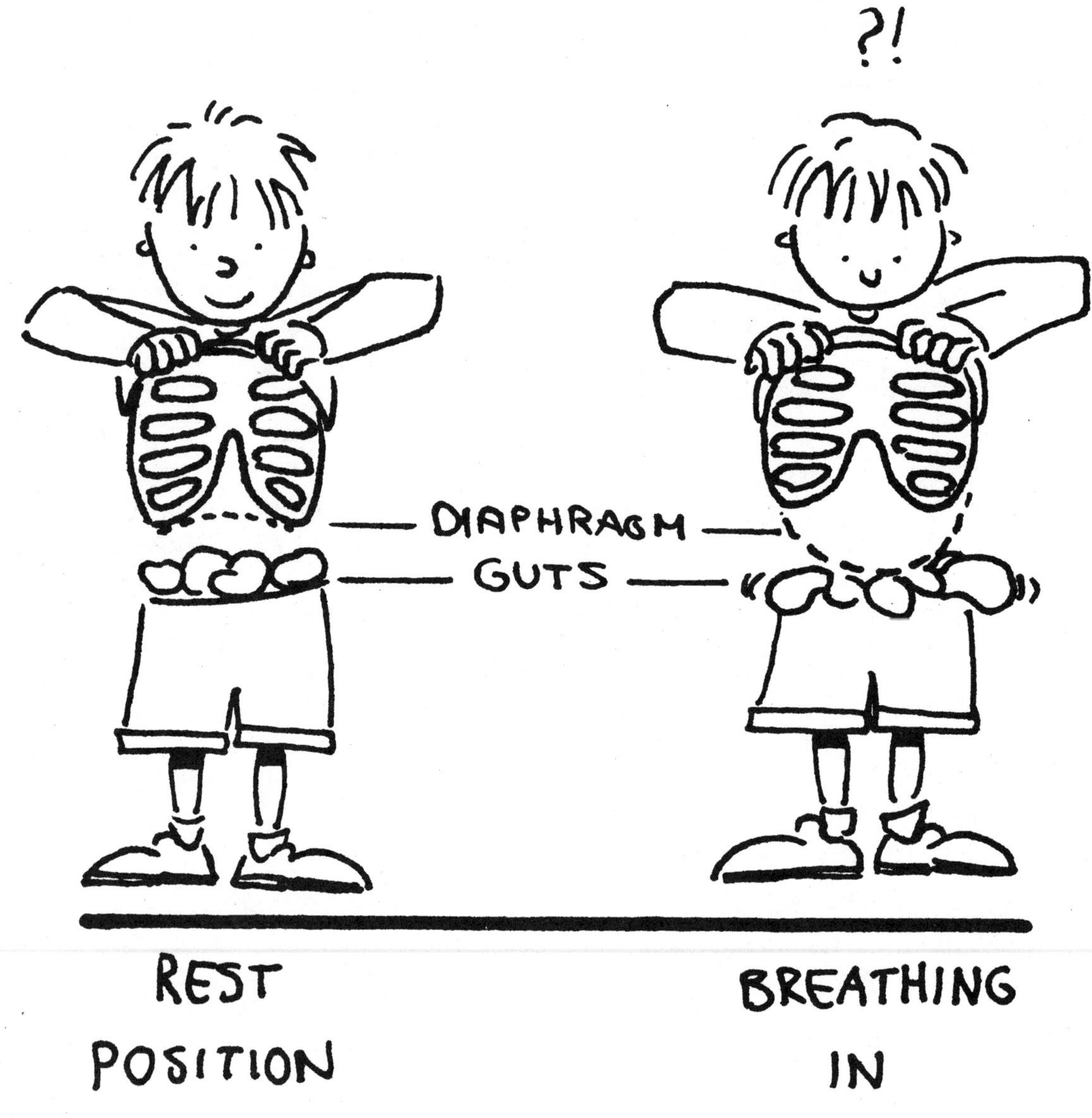

If you are lying down or reclining in an easy chair, you will sense the action of the diaphragm on a breath in, as it pushes the lower guts outward. Try placing your hand lightly on your abdomen as your body breathes in and out. You will feel pressure against your hand during inhalation (breath in) unless you tense your abdomen (don't do that!)

Sit up straight now, and wrap your fingers around the lower ribs on either side of your body to see if you can detect some of the horizontal expansion in the rib cage. Notice any breathing restrictions if you "slouch".

Sit up straight. Now, with your hand, feel the abdominal muscles do their work as you experiment with "hm" again: feel how the lower-guts squeeze in to start the vocal motor; then notice them relax and push out against your hand to let the new breath in as your diaphragm lowers.

Body Part #3:
The Vibrator: The Vocal Folds

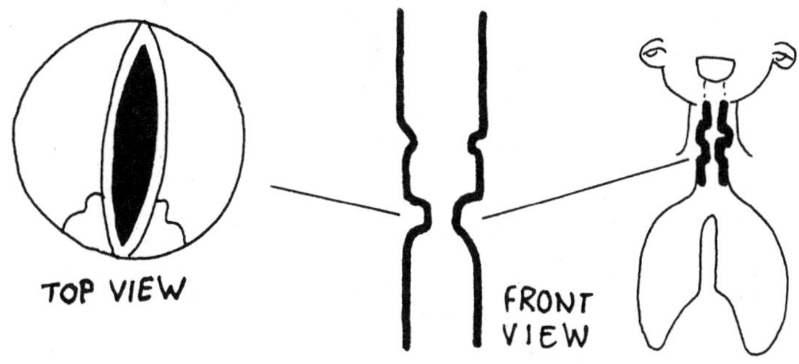

The vocal folds (also called "vocal cords") live in the voicebox or "larynx" at the top of the windpipe. It is rather difficult to imagine what they look like, so I am showing you two different views in the diagrams: the way they look from the front, and also from the top.

The two vocal folds are literally folds of muscle and skin that jut out into the airway. When they are pulled wide apart, the folds are in the correct position for breathing. When the muscles around them bring the vocal folds close together, they are in the correct position for vocalizing.

Since the vocal folds are part of the airway-protection system, they can also be used as a valve that closes very tightly. By squeezing together, the vocal folds help to keep any food or fluid out of the airway when we swallow, or to expel invading objects when we cough. When we need to push hard, we also close the vocal fold valve tightly to hold air in the lungs and give us more pushing power. The valving mechanism is a normal part of everyday functions (swallowing, coughing, pushing) that involve muscles common to the food-tube (esophagus) and the voicebox.

What happens when the airflow "fuel" hits the vocal folds?

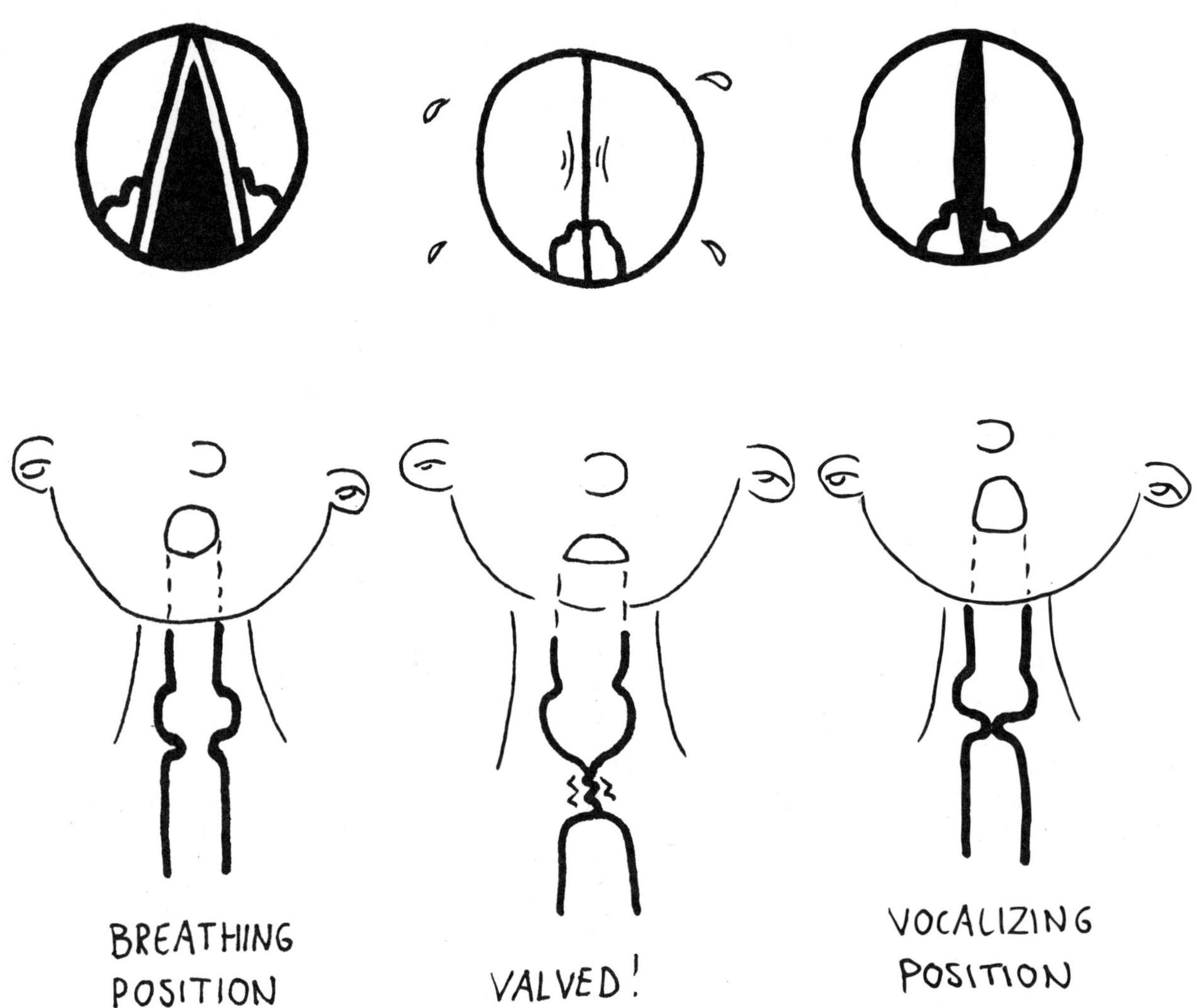

<table>
<tr>
<td>If the vocal folds are wide open, the airflow comes out as breath</td>
<td>If they are tightly closed, like during pushing, the air can't get out at all. (Try holding your breath, but trying to push the air out anyway.)</td>
<td>If the vocal folds are close together but not closed too tightly, they are set into wave-like vibration, as ocean water is set into vibration when the wind blows across it.</td>
</tr>
</table>

The vibrating movement of the vocal folds, described simply, is an alternate opening and closing of the vocal fold edges against each other. The result of this continuous opening/closing cycle is a disturbance of molecules in the air column that lives in the throat. This disturbance in the air is known as a "sound pressure wave" or simply "sound". Like the waves on the ocean on a windy day, the vibrating motion of the vocal folds is very complex. This is due to the constant interplay between air pressures, body tissues vibrating, and resonances and echoes in the throat and mouth.

It is fascinating to find out that the vocal folds open and close from 100 to 400 times per second during speech! ***("hm!")***

When we said "hm!" we caused the vocal folds to vibrate in the airstream for a brief time ...less than half a second. If we continue generating airflow with muscles in the breathing centre, we can sustain the vocal fold vibration: ***"hmmmmmmmmmmm..."***

The vocal commander (remember, *the brain?*) provides ongoing information to the breathing equipment and the voicebox about the meaning, importance and emotional intent of a speech message. By doing so, the commander dictates continual adjustments to the duration, pitch, loudness, and tone quality of speech, through muscle actions. These adjustments are largely sub-conscious. Let's explore this briefly with "hm":

> Try your sudden, brief "hm!" response for several different types of emotional reactions. Remember: don't plan *how* to do it, just respond spontaneously to the meaning:
>
> **"hm!"** (meaning: that's fascinating)
> **"hm!"** (meaning: sure, but who cares)
> **"hm!"** (meaning: that's the most ridiculous thing I've ever heard)

... A LITTLE EXPERIMENT WITH THE BREATHING AND VIBRATING EQUIPMENT:

HM! THAT'S FASCINATING!

Do you notice any differences in the degree or type of action in your breathing centre for the different meanings?
(correct answer: "yes")

Do you notice any differences in the type of sound you are producing for the different meanings?
(correct answer: "yes")

Body Part #4:
The Resonators: The Vocal Tract

Any cavity that a sound wave passes through can be a resonator. A resonator receives the sound wave and modifies it in ways that are determined by the size, shape and texture of the cavity.

For example, hitting a large glass jar with a spoon will create a different sound than hitting a small glass jar of the same shape and thickness with the same amount of force. The impact of the spoon causes the sound wave in each of the resonators (jars), but the resonators are different sizes.

Your personal vocal resonators include your throat, mouth, nose and face sinuses. Let's try an experiment with your voice and its resonators:

Say and hold out the sound **"ah"** with your jaw clenched.

Now say and hold out **"ah"** with your mouth wide open.

Are the sounds different?
(correct answer: "yes")

Do they feel different?
(correct answer: "yes")

How?...
(ah now, there is no simple answer to this question, so just respond intuitively)

You might be getting the impression that bigger cavities, like the large glass jar and your open mouth, make sounds stronger. We will be exploring ways to make this helpful principle work in the physical voice-improvement program.

Differences in speech sounds are due mainly to the changing shapes of the human resonator cavities, especially the mouth. When you say a vowel sound, you use the breathing equipment and the vibrator in much the same way, whether you say "ee"; "o"; "ay"; or "ah"... If you say these sounds in front of a mirror, you will see some obvious differences in the shape of the mouth resonator. How would you describe the differences?

Try comparing some other speech resonator shapes while looking in the mirror:

Say: **"i"; "oo"; "rrrr"; "mmmmm" ... FEEEEEEEEEL IT! ...**

Here's one more fact about resonance that is very important when you want to improve your voice. **Resonance is a physical property, therefore you can actually <u>feel</u> it:**

> If you put your fingers on your face while you say: **"hmmmmmmmmmm ..."**, you will feel a buzzing sensation.
>
> You may notice the resonance-buzz even without your finger, by paying attention to the way your nose, cheeks, lips or teeth feel when you hum. We'll be exploring this delightful phenomenon further in the physical program.

Body Part #5:

The Articulators: Mouth Pieces

Any moveable mouth or throat part could be a speech articulator. Here is a list of important mouth parts we use to talk:

TONGUE

LIPS

JAW

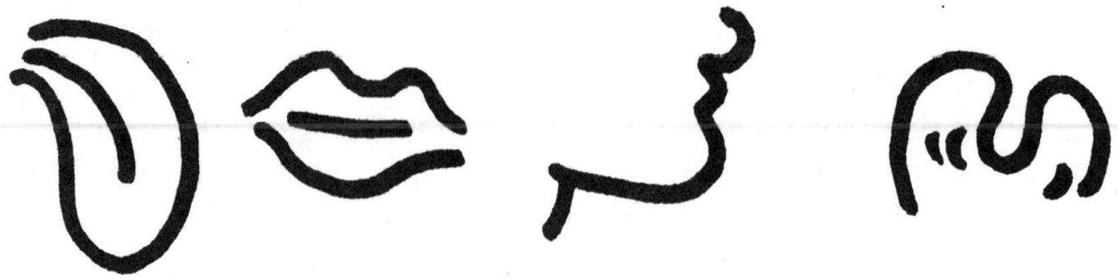

SOFT PALATE
(the soft part at the back of the roof of your mouth)

Whenever you move a mouth part like your tongue, and vocalize at the same time, you have articulated something: it may or may not be real speech.

Say: **"lalalalalala..."** in front of the mirror, and notice your tongue flapping up and down in your mouth on **"l"**.

You have just articulated some speech sounds (there was no meaning in it, so we can't assume you communicated anything).

Some speech sounds are articulated without vocalizing at all; instead they disturb airflow to make a "pop" or a "hiss":

Try: "p"; "t"; "ssssss"; "sh"; "ch" *(have a look in the mirror)*

In a way, the moveable mouth parts serve to "decorate" the flow of vocal tone from the vocal tract, and turn it into recognizable speech. This, of course is a very important function for human beings.

Have you ever tried to speak clearly after the dentist froze your tongue or lips? ... You can certainly still vocalize freely, but the articulators do not seem to do their job of producing different speech sounds in your mouth.

Body Part #6:

The Monitors: Ears and Other Body Sensors

When we talk, we tend to listen to ourselves to make sure our message is coming out right. The commander listens through our ears for signs that the words or vocal tone are not clear or true to the intended meaning; then it adjusts its commands for the rest of the message to clarify the intent.

The commander may also receive input from the eye sensors about the clarity of our message or emotional reaction of our listeners (do they look puzzled/angry/excited about what we are saying?).

Finally, the commander may receive signals from the muscle and resonance sensors about good or bad sensations during speech.

The body may be sending any number of signals to the commander:

"Ooww, this conversation is straining my throat!"

"I like the way these words are vibrating my palate!"

"If only my voice could be clear and free like it used to be!"

"Hm, I can feel the vocal power right here in my belly!"

"Yikes, how did that frog get in my throat?"

If any of our monitors are put out of commission the speech muscles may be commanded to make a special effort to be "heard".

For example, if your ears get plugged, or if you can't hear your own voice over noise, you will feel "pressured" to push your voice out so your monitors can hear it.

OHOH! HERE WE GO! THE DO'S AND THE DON'TS!
GUESS WHAT!? STAYING HEALTHY IS NOT ONLY GOOD FOR YOUR VOICE...
IT IS ALSO GOOD FOR YOUR HEALTH!

SECTION 2:
Your Voice and Your Health

Vocal Hygiene Means Cleaning Up Your Act!

Guess What!? Staying healthy is good for your voice! Now you know that talking is both a mental and a physical activity. If you're unwell or tired, all physical and mental activities are more difficult to start and finish. You need energy to think and organize what you're going to say; you need energy to make the equipment work well, and you need energy to monitor and correct your message.

So here's your first rule-set for keeping a healthy voice:

1. Make sure you get adequate rest and sleep every day, including several periods of rest for your voice.

2. Exercise your whole body daily; enough to keep energy flowing and keep your mind sharp, but not so much that you're too tired to think and talk.

3. Don't use your voice extensively when you're over-tired or sick.

4. Eat healthy foods that agree with you, and don't overeat.

5. Drink plenty of water, and other non-caffeinated, non-alcoholic fluids: remember 8-10 glasses per day for most full-grown people (more if you're hot or very physically active).

6. Stay away from foods, fluids and chemicals that dehydrate the body, give you heartburn or gas, make your throat feel tight or "gummy"; make you cough and clear your throat:

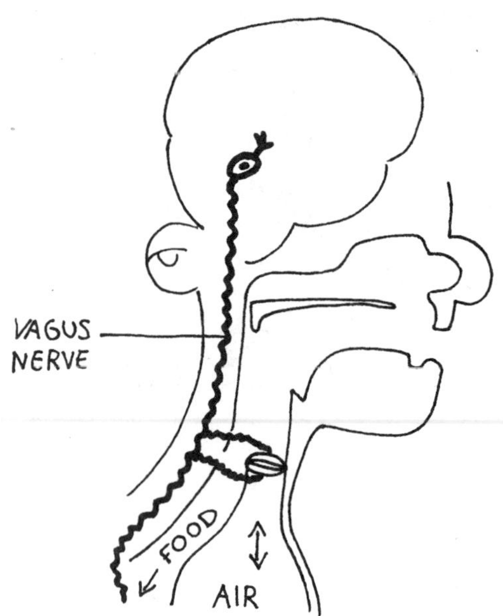

In some people, eating habits contribute to throat and voice problems by creating excessive stomach acid, or causing it to leak out of the stomach. This can result in heartburn or indigestion; but sometimes acid leaks are felt at the top of the esophagus (food-tube) and in the voicebox as well. This occurs because the esophagus and voicebox are joined at the top, have muscles in common, and are both "commanded" through the "Vagus Nerve". The voicebox reacts by valving to protect the airway from acid leaks. The resulting sensations in the throat may be mistaken as "allergies", "post-nasal drip" or "asthma".

The most common throat reactions to stomach acid leaks are: froggy or foggy morning voice, feeling a lump or phlegm in the throat, throat-clearing and coughing. These symptoms are accentuated by overeating, eating before going to bed, eating before exercising, certain types of foods and drinks, being overweight, lifting heavy objects, and being stressed. Other activities that might cause acid leaks: bending over (like when you are gardening); hanging upsidedown; bunjie-jumping

POTENTIAL NO-NO FOODS, DRINKS and CHEMICALS: caffeine; nicotine; alcohol; fatty-rich foods; spicy foods; acidic foods and drinks

If you suspect you have this type of leaky-acid throat problem you should consult with your doctor about it!

THE VOICEBOX AS A VALVE:

Certain vocal activities occur when we use the voicebox as a valve. Remember that the voicebox is the natural closing system to separate the food tube from the airway. When we cough, throat-clear, push or lift heavy objects (even weights in the gym), we use the voicebox as a valve. In this state, the vocal folds do not vibrate easily: there is a lot of tension in the throat when it is valving, so it is a terrible time to vocalize!

If you are a habitual throat-clearer or cougher, try to catch yourself before you "attack" your voice this way; better yet, have friends and family members alert you to this abusive habit that you may not even be aware of... Have a sip of water or hum gently instead of beating up on your vocal folds with a throat-clear! Check with your doctor about potential "acid leaks".

VOCALIZING AND EXERCISING:

Like coughing and clearing your throat, certain **"grunting"** noises we make during exercise may be harmful to the voice, because they are valving noises. **You may need to modify your exercise regime to keep your voice healthy!**

Talking during strenuous aerobic exercise is also not a good idea: you will find that breathing for exercise and breathing for speech are quite different and incompatible. **After exercising, you should wait until your breathing system can function in its capacity as vocal-energy generator.**

Even walking and talking at the same time can be detrimental to your voice: the most important consideration is: **where** are you walking? If you're strolling along a city street, you may be competing with noise that will make you strain your voice.

NICOTINE: NUMBER 1 ENEMY OF THE VOICE!

If you're not already convinced that **smoking is bad, bad, bad** for your voice, remember that over 90% of cancers of the lungs and voicebox are related to smoking! The combination of chemicals and nicotine can make the cells lining your voicebox and lungs change in uncontrolled ways, causing swelling, pre-cancerous and cancerous tumours. **If you're a smoker, the nicest thing you can do for your voice immediately, is QUIT!**

NOISE: #2 ENEMY OF THE VOICE!

One of the voice's other worst enemies is noise. When the ear-monitors hear noise, they tell the brain that it will have to "gear-up" and push the voice equipment to over-ride the noise. Noise is annoying when it competes with our important message, so we tend to tense our throat muscles, apply valving forces, and push to get the message out. If we talk in noisy areas often, the unconscious brain may ignore the interference: to the point that we are not even aware of straining our voices.

Here are some common sources of speech-competing noises: *people talking, yelling or singing; people moving around; people playing musical instruments or with noisy toys; traffic or engine noises (cars, buses, airplanes, trains); office equipment; power tools; heating/air-conditioning systems; household appliances (dishwasher, TV, radio...)*

Can you think of some additional sources of speech-competing noises in your life?

SECTION 3:
Your Voice, Your Emotions and Your Personality

Your personality and self-image are reflected in the way you use your voice. This connection may be good or bad for your voice...

If you are an outgoing and talkative person, who seeks out situations to share your thoughts with other people, you probably have lots of energy most of the time to drive the vocal equipment. However, if your desire to be with other people runs your life, you may find you devote very little time to resting your voice, and the equipment may show signs of overuse: hoarseness, voice breaks or feeling of strain. Let's say your job also demands that you talk extensively; maybe your work environment is noisy, so you must strain your voice when you use it on the job. If you also enjoy lively atmospheres, you may find yourself socializing in loud environments where lots of voices, music, and other noises compete with your message...

On the other hand, if you're a shy or low-energy person, you may have designed your life in a way so your talking is minimal. Sometimes recruiting the energy and self-confidence to do the necessary talking for your job or other life activities may feel like a burden. You may have discovered you're a magnet for outgoing people..."the quiet listener who never interrupts". They may comment: "My, it's been nice talking with you!"

Some people would like to sound like someone different than they really are: for example a man with a natural tenor voice (like Pavarotti) might decide to talk with a deeper voice, because it makes him feel more masculine and authoritative. This may prove useful in some situations, but may be very hard on the vocal equipment. It may make him overtax the system, like driving a car at the wrong speed in the wrong gear.

Unfortunately, many cultural and social influences may entice us to imitate certain people's voices that we admire: the booming voice of a radio-announcer; the soft, alluring voice of an attractive actor; the bright, cheery voice of a popular friend...

The vocal result of imitation is rarely successful, and can result in vocal strain. If you are attempting to emanate a voice-idol, some serious soul-searching may be necessary for you to recognize and accept that you are not using your "real" voice.

On the other hand, if you are aspiring to make a "big impression" that will yield fame and wealth, you should seek a qualified vocal trainer who can help you achieve the desired effects without straining your voice.

It is natural that your voice should reflect how you are feeling at any given time. If you are feeling happy and excited, your voice equipment should respond naturally with lots of energy and inflection. If you're feeling angry, your vocal energy should express tones that present the emotion energetically and explosively. If you're feeling unhappy, shy, sick or tired, your voice may be low in energy and pitch, monotone...

When we were very young, we manipulated our small worlds by expressing our emotions freely: vocally and physically. As our social world expanded, we adopted more "adult" ways of manipulating our people-environment: by revealing our emotions very selectively, and when necessary, holding back the true feelings by squeezing the muscles of our throat, breathing system, mouth and face. By keeping our voices controlled, low and monotone, we endeavour to hide our true feelings as we talk.

As our personalities develop and are influenced by society, we learn that responding emotionally to certain situations may not help us get what or where we want: we learn to edit our words and hide our real feelings with our voices. We may often hold back the instinctive physical responses that would express strong emotions: crying; screaming or yelling.

We may often feel a pressure to "put on a happy face" to protect ourselves from revealing negative emotions.

The forced social smile is adopted in many work environments where it does not necessarily reflect the true feelings of the workers. It may even "help us" ignore our emotional instincts, by tensing and immobilizing the muscles of spontaneous facial expression. By talking through a forced smile we stiffen our lips and jaw to prevent emotional outbursts. Tension in this part of the face is transmitted automatically to the voicebox, so our voices will be tense and stiff when our faces are tense and stiff. If we put on the "happy face" too often, we may forget to take it off again!

SECTION 4:

Your Voice and Your Job

Your job may demand that you talk or sing extensively, sometimes under high stress, in unhealthy postures, and often in noisy areas, or rooms with very poor acoustic features. These working conditions can result in constant muscle tension in the face, neck, breathing equipment, voicebox... Result?: voice strain, hoarseness, voice breaks, **frustration!** The harder you try and the more you worry about your voice, the worse it gets.

Fixing the problem may require that you take a complete environmental inventory, adjusting your work-space and noise interference as much as possible, and changing the way you respond vocally to do your job. *Yikes! This sounds overwhelming!* So, let's break it down into logical steps:

ACOUSTIC ENVIRONMENT:

We've already discussed the effect that noise can have on vocal effort. You may be aware of intermittent noises that make you push your voice (of course, you stop talking until they subside, right!)... you may be unaware of continuous noises that your ears have learned to "block out": noisy fans, office equipment, etc. The sub-conscious brain still "hears" it, so tells you to push and strain over that annoying buzz or whir.

If your job involves gaining people's attention to demonstrate or explain a point, **your voice will thank you if you find non-vocal ways to alert and silence your listeners, so you don't have to compete with their noise while you impart your knowledge.** Bells, whistles, clapping, hand signals, lights on-off, music ... have all been used successfully to signal to an "audience" that you need their undivided attention and silence.

A poor acoustic environment is the insidious enemy of the voice: large spaces; echoes and environmental noise are common culprits. Your ear monitors and the poor attention of an audience may alert you to the fact that your message is not coming through "loud and clear". This realization inevitably makes you strain to hear your own voice.

The golden rule is: **if you can't hear your voice well using a normal conversational level, you will need some electronic help to amplify the sound.** This means you should use a personal amplification system that is adequate for your vocal projection needs. The system should be powerful enough to compensate for room size and acoustics (the larger the room and the poorer the acoustics, the more power you will need). The system should have a monitoring device that provides you with immediate information about how well the amplifier is doing its job. If you can hear your voice message coming back clearly to you from the speakers, your volume gain is adequate and you will stop straining to be heard. You could shop for this type of system in a professional sound-equipment or music store.

POSTURE POINTERS:

The work environment can be full of hazards to healthy posture. The position of your telephone, computer screen, keyboard, desk, chair or reading materials relative to your body parts will influence how you sit, stand, and work. Your work "props" may cause you to pull your head back, stick your chin out, twist your neck, raise your shoulders, curve your back... slouch!

> *If your computer screen is higher than eye level, you may correct for this by straining your chin forward to direct your eyes upward; if your keyboard sits high on your desk, you may pull your fingers up from your shoulders to type; If you need your glasses to read, but must peer above them to see in the distance, you may pull your head back on your neck and strain your neck forward to look beyond your reading material.*

Since your speech equipment lives in your body, healthy posture is a prerequisite to healthy voice production. We will be exploring posture habits and rediscovering healthy posture in the physical program, as a first step toward vocalizing with ease.

SCHEDULING YOUR VOICE USE AND VOICE REST:

This may sound too obvious to put into print, but here goes: **your voice needs rest periods just as any other body equipment does!**

Would you spend your entire day dancing or running without training to prepare for such a marathon? Of course you wouldn't! Would you stretch and rest to recover from the muscle fatigue and cramps afterwards? Of course you would! Since our speech equipment comprises so many body parts, it is not surprising that it gets "tired" and "uncooperative" when we demand vocal marathon performances.

Have you ever been so tired your legs and feet "forget" how to walk properly? The brain and body parts involved in speaking are more numerous and complex than those for most other daily physical functions... so imagine how much concentration and energy is required to keep the speech equipment responding all day in a coordinated, efficient and coherent manner!

You will find it easier to keep the speech equipment responding efficiently if you can schedule your periods of heavy vocal demand apart. If you have any say-so about when vocally-demanding meetings or classes are scheduled, don't book them back-to-back. Give yourself time to re-group, re-think, and re-energize!

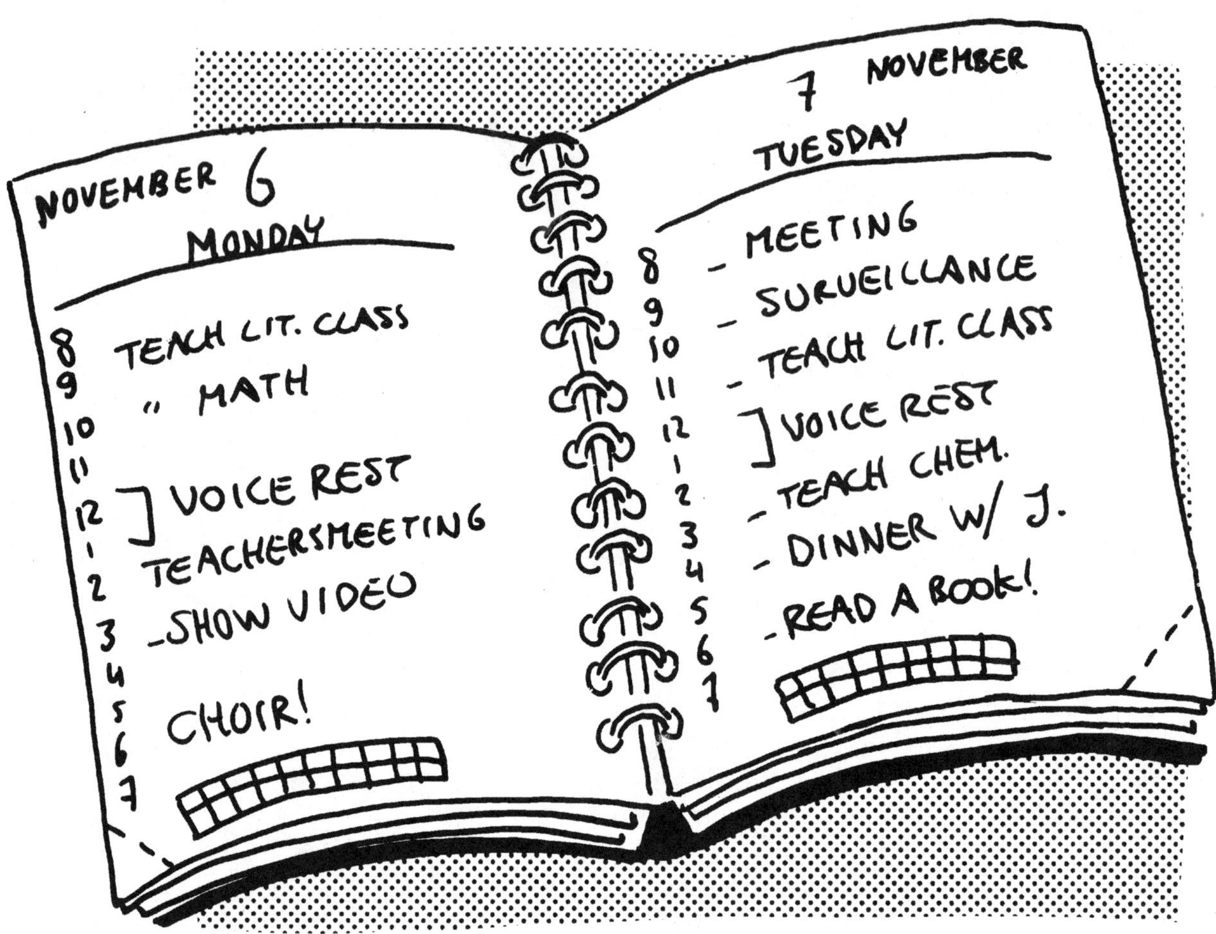

SCHEDULE YOUR VOICE USE!

If you can't avoid back-to-back vocal "performances", plan your presentation carefully to allow for appropriate turn-taking, pauses, and non-vocal activities. Remember, people absorb information better if they are stimulated through a variety of input channels, and if they are directly involved in a meeting or class, rather than passive information "sponges".

If you feel your presentation or teaching strategies could use some polishing, consider participating in a course on public speaking, teaching techniques, or meeting management. Effective presentation tactics are designed to help you impart information efficiently while maximizing your audience's attention and participation. Once you are a skilled public speaker, you will be able to economize on vocalizing time and effort.

The Plight of Teachers:

Today's teachers face a major challenge: how to be good facilitators of learning while overcoming the environmental "hazards" to good vocal performance, and coping with the stresses created by population explosions, expectations of students/parents/society, and political and administrative fluctuations? As teachers we perform, explain, justify, intervene, negotiate, emote, repress ... all in a day's work. We often feel that every activity demands our vocal input.

Since it is difficult to be a teacher without a voice, we must plan our curricula with vocal health in mind; avoid using our voices to command attention; assess the vocal hazards in our environment; rally for the best possible speaking conditions; and maybe even swallow our pride and use electronic amplification when competing noises cannot be suppressed. Perhaps we should incorporate vocal health programs into our teaching curricula!

SECTION 5:
Your Voice and Your Life

Family, friends, hobbies, goals, dreams, in other words, your life: can place demands on your time and voice use that push you to your vocal limits or beyond. The last thing your voice needs after a long busy day of talking at the office is to converse over dinner in a noisy restaurant, chair a committee meeting, or coach your son's soccer team!

Your pursuit of stardom as a singer may stand in the way of, or be hampered by your occupational voice use as a teàcher, customer service representative, trial lawyer, switchboard operator, swimming instructor, waiter or other vocally-demanding job. **As with other time and energy-consuming activities of life, you may need to subject your vocally-demanding activities to some serious priority planning.** If pursuing your dream to sing your way to fame is all-consuming, your interim wage-earning activities best not involve much vocalizing, especially in a noisy environment. If your occupational salary is dependent on a reliable voice, your leisure activities best not involve vocally abusive behaviours like yelling, screaming, or singing raucously.

SPEECH AND HEARING

If you communicate frequently with individuals experiencing a hearing loss or other comprehension challenges, you need to take extra precautions that you do not strain your voice to be heard, nor set yourself up for constant repetitions of your message.

Here are some handy tips for optimizing communication with someone who is hearing-impaired or has difficulty understanding:

1. Wait until you are sure you have your communication partner's attention before you begin the conversation. You could touch him/her on the arm, tap on the table, wave a signal or try other ways to make sure your listener is alert and ready.

2. Make sure you and your communication partner are always facing each other, and that you are close enough, and the lighting adequate so your faces are visible to each other. (We all tend to "speech-read" or "lip-read" when we have the opportunity, since it provides valuable information that can clarify speech.)

3. Do not attempt to have a conversation with someone while you are in a moving vehicle, other noisy environments, or other situations where you are not facing each other.

4. Keep your hands and other obstructions away from your face.

5. Speak clearly without exaggerating your speech movements. Don't rush your speech. Pause frequently, and verify that your message is understood often so you can both enjoy a meaningful conversation.

6. Use natural speech inflections: don't exaggerate, but don't speak in a monotone.

7. Turn OFF the radio, TV, household appliances, and other noisemakers before you begin a conversation.

TALKING TO YOUR COMPUTER: the Latest Technology-Generated Problem

If you are dependent on a hands-free speech-activated computer program to communicate (or to get your work done), you may have experienced one of the most technically-challenging demands on your voice. Voice-activated software is relatively new and inflexible.

> *We have had to adapt our speech patterns to accommodate the current technology, because the computer is unable to adapt to our naturally variable and fluent speech patterns. Whenever you need to adjust a physical activity like your speech pattern quickly, it is susceptible to misuse. Since computers are not as smart as people, they may require that you separate each word, and use certain vocal "effects" to recognize what you are saying.*

You may find yourself using the valving system in your speech to create distinct word boundaries, sharp "vocal attacks", or unnatural stress or inflection patterns. You will probably find you can create all the required vocal effects to communicate successfully with your computer if you optimize your vocal production with the physical program that follows. If you are having difficulty applying these techniques effectively, you should consult with your speech-language pathologist and/or communications specialist. Hopefully in time, our computers will be smart enough to interpret what we say without our need to compromise natural speech patterns and flow.

HAMMERING OUT SOME "BUGS" IN THE NEW SOFTWARE!

SECTION 6:
The Physical Program

Now that you understand how voice functions in the context of your life, it's time to learn how to make your speech equipment work naturally, so you can VOCALIZE with EASE ...

THE PHILOSOPHY OF PRACTICE:

The primary responsibility for your voice improvement belongs to *you.* Busy people like you generally find it difficult to add yet another chore to the daily routine, so we will try to find meaningful ways to incorporate the important changes into your life. Seek support and cooperation from the individuals you communicate with regularly. You may be amazed to learn how many people wish they could vocalize with ease!

Here's some good news: the good patterns you will <u>practice regularly</u> are SIMPLE, SIMPLE, SIMPLE and EASY, EASY, EASY! The body responds best to simple instructions that create rewarding changes we can feel, see, or hear immediately.

The Physical Program is based on a powerful philosophy governing the acquisition of new motor patterns:

> *Your current speech habits are largely sub-conscious. They consist of well established brain-to-nerve-to-muscle patterns. Your body may offer feedback about the inappropriateness of certain "bad" habits ("Ouch, this hurts my throat"; "Oh dear, my voice is tired"; "How did that frog get in my throat?"), but your speech equipment is programmed to operate in the wrong way: the way you talked yesterday is the way you'll talk today, and tomorrow, and the next day ... unless you make a conscious effort to interrupt the undesirable patterns and replace them with "good" ones. You begin this process with some simple exercises. However, you can't expect the body to adopt the good patterns after just a few trials (even if they are really more natural and healthy). You need to interrupt the bad habits so often that the body re-programs your speech responses so they include only the good patterns.*

Now for some more good news: your body is naturally hard-wired to operate the speech equipment in the healthy way ... So, when you practice healthy vocal behaviours, you are really re-introducing something familiar to your body: an inborn easy speech pattern.

Still more good news: vocalizing naturally will feel good, and sound good, and look good, even if at first it is not recognizable to your monitors. It will take your monitors time to adapt to speech patterns that feel and sound different than what they're accustomed to, even if the feedback from your sensors is positive.

During the physical program, you will become familiar with three stages of reforming your speech patterns:

A. EXPLORING AND DISCOVERING the bad habits that your body has adopted, and the healthy, natural patterns that allow you to vocalize with ease;

B. RE-PROGRAMMING THE SYSTEM by rehearsing simple exercises regularly, so that healthy patterns become familiar and begin to replace the bad habits;

C. HABITUALIZING the healthy patterns so they are reflected in all your speech and vocalizing activities.

Physical Program Step 1:

Naturalizing Your Posture

Barring any physical problems, **natural healthy posture was a gift you were born with.** No one had to teach you how to align your spine or balance your head on your neck to master standing and walking. No one had to tell you not to slouch: that behaviour was simply not in your posture repertoire during your early years. *In fact, if you had been slouching when you first tried to sit, stand or walk, you might still be crawling around on all fours!* We are hard-wired for perfect posture at birth: you only need observe the naturally erect profile of a baby sitting, standing, or taking his first steps to realize that bad posture is an "acquired" behaviour.

Good posture means natural relationships among the various body parts. I don't know many adults who are still experiencing "good" posture without some conscious attention to the basics.

A. EXPLORE AND DISCOVER:

"How can I rediscover the natural alignment I was born with?"

The following equipment will come in handy for this part of the physical program:

- a slightly padded floor or carpet
- a full-length mirror
- a straight wall
- a chair with a straight back and a flat seat (the chair's seat, that is)
- a book (any book with thickness of ¾" - 1")
- a leotard, or other apparel that allows you to examine your posture honestly
- a video-camera, if you are a technology buff

DOCTOR, I SEE NOTHING WRONG WITH MY POSTURE!
CAN I GO NOW?

A good way to start examining your every-day posture is to consult with your physical monitors. Posture monitors include the eyes, muscles, and pain sensors.

Let's start by consulting the eye-monitors. Find your full-length mirror and place it strategically close so you can glance at yourself with a front and side view. Once you have a good objective view of your body, look away for awhile, and engage yourself in some activity like reading, talking on the phone, watching TV, working on your computer. Without changing your alignment, glance back in the mirror, and describe what you see.

– SELFREFLECTION –

Check for: **straightness or curviness of your back and neck**
relationship between your neck and head
angle of your head
position of your shoulders
position of your legs relative to one another

Try spying on your body in both standing and sitting positions, for several different activities and locations (working in your office; "hanging around" in the living room; eating or cooking in the kitchen; goofing around in the back-yard)

Does what you see remind you more of "homo erectus" or "homo slouchus"? Can you make specific comments about alignment areas that are okay, or need correcting?

VISUAL OBSERVATIONS ABOUT MY POSTURE: ______________________________

____

____

(If you enjoy hi-tech, have a video-camera spy on you and discreetly document your posture in some typical situations)

Let's turn to the muscles and pain monitors now. These monitors will tell you about areas of muscle strain, tension, and spasm if you pay close attention to them. Try spying on your muscles from your feeling sensors, in some typical situations of your life. Contrast the sensations in relaxed situations with those you feel when you are intensely engaged in some activity.

Check for: **stiffness or pain in your neck, shoulders, back**
breathing effort
general uneasiness or muscle twitching
headache
muscle strain or fatigue
jaw clenching
face tension
throat tension

Try to be as specific as possible about the location of tense or sore areas. See if you can relate this report to your eye monitor's report and your current visual observations (are you still in front of the mirror?).

Good posture provides us with a nice-looking and nice-feeling body. It also ensures maximum freedom for all the body's moving parts: head, neck, shoulders, elbows, wrists, finger joints, breathing system, legs...

Maximum freedom of body parts gives us potential for flexibility and power when we perform physical activities like talking. Good posture is dynamic: a constantly adjusting system that improves mobility, ***not*** a set of positions. Good posture makes vocalizing EASY!

Now let's begin applying some principles of natural, dynamic body posture:

Use your mirror to "back up" your observations: As you stand, your head, neck and back are *aligned:* an imaginary line passes through your body from the crown of the head through the back of the neck and centre back...

SKELETON-SUSPENSION:

Imagine your skeleton is suspended from the crown of the head. Gravity helps your torso, arms and legs fall away from the head in a natural alignment: your body grows taller because of the gentle upward pull from the suspension force.

As your head is gently pulled upward, it is released from the top of your neck. Prove this by gently shaking it in a "no" gesture. Imagine you are drawing a 2 centimetre horizontal line with your nose. Make the movement small and loose and confine it to your head. The big neck muscles should not be assisting.

As your head is gently pulled upward, make a teeter-toter movement with it: like nodding "yes". Imagine you are drawing a 2 centimetre vertical line with your nose. As with "no", the "yes" gesture is very small and free. It confirms that you have liberated your head from your neck and spine.

HELIUM-HEAD:

Pretend your head is a helium balloon. It is attached to the rest of the body by a very delicate string that is the neck and spine. Let the light helium gas draw your head up off your neck-string, to provide the spine-lengthening effect. If a gentle breeze comes up, you will feel your helium-head float about in space.

HIGH ON HELIUM!

Fun with Gravity:

You might enjoy some activities that allow you to play with gravity: *(take turns reading the instructions to each other: one person instructs, while the other indulges in the exercise)*

RELAXATION: *Aaaaahhhhh...*

Find a nice spot on your carpet to lie on your back. Rest your head on a book that is 3/4" - 1" thick. This allows you to gently stretch the back of the neck as you release the head away from your body.

Indulge in relaxation for a few minutes, as your body gives in to gravity. Let your body monitors tell you what it feels like to relax, as you rediscover natural alignment. Take time to feel the individual parts of your body becoming heavy. Notice how little resistance your body offers gravity in this position.

Notice how gravity pushes air out of the body during the out-flowing breath-tide. Allow your spine to lengthen along the floor.

EASY WALKING:

You can also use gravity in upright positions, standing or sitting, to relax the body and free individual body parts: feel the effect of gravity on your shoulders, arms, legs, and breathing equipment. Take your body for a little walk using the imaginary suspension rope (or helium) to release your head and lengthen your spine, and using gravity to keep your arms and legs free and mobile.

THE HEAD-BALL and THE NECK-POST:

While sitting or standing, balance your "head-ball" on the very top of your "neck-post". Very **delicately** and **slowly** tip your head-ball backward, until you feel its weight begin to transfer back, and gravity taking over. **Do not jerk the head backward suddenly!**

Take your time, and tune in to your posture monitors. Once you feel the weight transferring, roll your head-ball carefully back up and re-balance it on top of your neck-post.

Notice the relative lightness of your head-ball once it is perched on top of the neck-post (remind you of a helium balloon?)

As you practice this exercise repeatedly, you should notice that the degree of movement required for you to feel the head-ball weight shifting in the direction of the tilt becomes smaller and smaller. When you become an expert at releasing your head-ball from your neck-post, you will find the movement is barely visible before you feel gravity taking over.

Repeat this exercise with your head-ball tipping forward, then to either side. Remember not to use any exaggerated or jerky movements! The displacement of your head-ball will be very small if you are truly releasing it from your neck-post before you begin, and if you are tuned in to your posture monitors.

Once your head-ball is re-balanced on top of your neck-post, notice it wants to be adjusting constantly with your movements. This confirms that you have liberated your head from your neck, and you are using "dynamic" posture.

Use "yes/no" nods and gravity-play with your head-ball frequently to confirm freedom between your head and neck.

Freeing the Upper Limbs and Torso:

WIGGLE AND SHAKE:

With your head-ball perched delicately on the very top of your neck-post, wiggle and shake your upper arms very gently at the shoulder joints. Use small movements to confirm the upper limbs have been liberated from your chest and back. When the shoulders are released away from the neck, your chest and back will be free and naturally wide. In standing position, your hands will fall just forward of the centre line in your legs, with palms facing inward. Feel how heavy and free the arms are when your body releases them from the neck and shoulders.

DO THE "V" THING:

To banish the homo slouchus within, start with your helium-head floating upward; arms dropped at your sides.

With your head still floating up and away from the neck, slowly raise your arms from the sides of your body, palms facing the ceiling. Raise them to the sides of your head, until your arms form a "V" with the palms of your hands facing each other.

Drop your arms back to the sides of your body. Feel the natural expansion across your chest: more room to breathe. Repeat several times.

HANG-OUT: *(WARNING: If you have back or neck problems, do this exercise only under the advice of your physical therapist or physician!)*

From sitting position, drop your heavy head-ball gently forward toward your chest, and drop your arms heavily to the sides of your body. **"Hang-out":** let the weight of your head and arms stretch your neck and back to release tension. Breathe gently into your back, and feel the muscles relax with each breath. Roll the spine back into upright position gently from bottom-to-top: the head-ball rolls up to the top of the neck-post last.

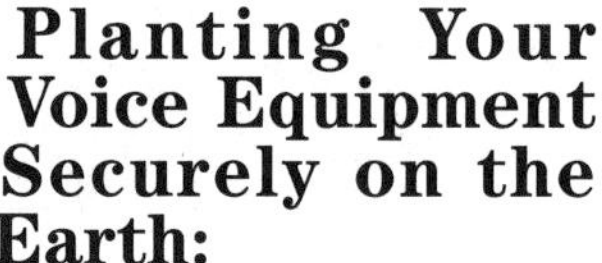

Planting Your Voice Equipment Securely on the Earth:

When you are standing to speak, you will want to take extra precautions to ensure your voice equipment is secure:

Plant your two feet firmly on the earth. Do not subject your voice equipment to precarious or high heels: this will throw your body alignment off-balance (and squish your toes!).

Let the weight of your whole body distribute itself evenly through the legs and feet. Keep your feet parallel to each other, and a comfortable and stable distance apart. Keep your knees loose and ready for action.

Allow your helium-head to float high above the neck-string and the rest of the voice equipment. Allow your spine to lengthen, back and chest to reach their natural width.

Keep your shoulders free of the neck and torso, arms loose and ready for action.

Do not hold your breath or clench your abdominal muscles.

In other words: stand comfortably and naturally tall! Seek out your muscle monitors and your mirror for advice and confirmation: they will tell you the truth if you let them!

The Use and Misuse of Furniture:

Much of our furniture is designed for casual sitting or lounging. With the exception of ergonomic office furniture, the chairs you subject your speech equipment to may hinder natural dynamic posture. The same principles of body alignment and freedom you used for standing apply to sitting.

How to avoid or cope with furniture that undermines healthy posture? Here are some guidelines and suggestions:

If you have the option of selecting new furniture, choose chairs that are adjustable for seat height, back-support, and arm-rest height. Choose a seat size that allows you to sit fully against the back support, and still bend your knees comfortably. Your feet should rest flat on the floor. The back support should do that: support your back when you are sitting upright. Some office chairs have back supports that move with you, so if you pivot forward, your back can stay straight. A chair with wheels will allow you to slide your legs under your desk.

If you are stuck with chairs that do not fit your body well, use cushions, back supports, foot-stools and other accessories to help you maintain healthy posture. You should be able to rest your lower and mid back comfortably against the back of the chair or chair-cushion, and still be able to bend your knees. Many casual chairs have a backward slope on the back-rest. Use cushions or back-supports to allow you to sit straight with adequate lower back support, but without a backward lean. Your feet should touch the floor or rest comfortably on a foot-rest. The chair seat should be horizontal and slightly padded for comfort.

Make sure your table or desk allows you to pull your chair up underneath, with ample leg room below the work surface. You should position yourself and your chair as close to the table as possible. The height of the table should accommodate your body size, so you do not have to raise your shoulders or elbows to work on the surface. Consider a desk that will allow you several surface heights: a low one for the computer keyboard, a higher one to allow your computer screen to rest at eyelevel.

If you spend much time reading, drawing or writing, you can buy or create a table surface that slants up away from you to support your work material without requiring you to slouch over it (a few bricks and a piece of plywood will do if aesthetics don't matter)

Once you have selected or corrected your furniture, position your most frequently-used work "props" close enough so that you don't have to reach beyond comfortable arm's length: place the phone close to you if you use it frequently; do the same with work tools, eating and drinking utensils.

Avoid "jaw-jut": the position change your body makes most frequently is probably a shift from sitting back against the chair to leaning forward to bring you closer to your work, props or conversation partner. This shift should be made from the crown of the head (head floating upward, back and neck lengthening, shoulders and back wide). The best way to make this position shift is to pivot from the hip-joint, while you maintain your natural alignment. You should feel as though you grow taller as you tilt forward; rather than slouching and shrinking:

All graceful and healthy movements are initiated from the crown of the head, not the chin. **Beware of the nasty alternative: "jaw-jut". Your eye monitors will catch it in the mirror: as you attempt to position your body forward, your chin pushes up and out, your neck curves forward, and your head strains backward: if you stay in this jaw-dictated posture, you may end up with a big pain in your neck!** Many people use jaw-jut subconsciously when they are in a confidential pose for conversation. The jaw and chest are thrust forward, the back and neck are bent tensely, and the voice-box is pulled high in the neck by the jaw: **OUCH!**

OK: Rest back against your vertical chair support, pull your chair closer to your listener if you wish, release your head-ball upward off your neck-post, let your back and neck lengthen; when you need to bring your face closer, use the hip-joint to pivot, and gently and naturally lengthen your spine...

The forward pivot is the first step in changing position from sitting to standing or standing to sitting. It will take some awareness and practice to accomplish these motions without "jaw-jut". Remember, the action begins with a release of the head from the neck and natural lengthening of the spine: the crown of the head dictates the upward and forward direction of movement: don't let the jaw take over!

More Hazards to Healthy Posture:

Vision-correcting glasses can be a hazard to healthy posture: if you tend to position your head stiffly and strain your neck to see over or under your glasses or bifocal line, your voice can suffer the consequences. If you are having difficulty adjusting to eye-ware, consult your optician to see if the correction can be made in a way that allows you to apply healthy posture principles during your visually-intensive activities.

The telephone has gone through major evolutionary stages. Now we can talk to our friends, associates or almost anyone while walking or driving down the street, while we wait for our lunch, and while we type memos into our computer. But wait: how does this marriage between our ear and our hand-held (or shoulder-held) phone leave our posture? Your trusty mirror can tell you exactly how your phone rules your body while you talk. If you are a "phoneoholic", or must hold a receiver while talking, walking, driving, typing, or otherwise being distracted from healthy body alignment, consider purchasing a head-set receiver or speaker-set to leave your hands-free while you communicate. You will find you can practice all the principles of natural dynamic alignment if you take this liberating step: after all this is the 20th century!

THE EVOLUTION OF THE TELEPHONE: THINGS ONLY GOT BETTER!

If you talk to your computer or dictation machine, make sure your microphone is placed well so your voice equipment is not subjected to "jaw-jut" or other neck strain. The ideal microphone is one that attaches to a head-set, so you can maintain healthy posture and keep your hands free while you dictate.

Take a Posture Break:

Whatever your work or hobbies, you will probably find you become "positioned" for extended periods during certain intense activities. If your posture is not dynamic during an activity, muscle stiffness and cramps can set in. Invite your pain monitors into your life at these times, and let common sense reign: if you have been holding your head, neck, back, arms, or other body parts in a specific position, take a break; release the muscles; determine the direction of the posture bias and try a gentle stretch in the opposite direction. If the posture-biasing activities coincide with extended periods of talking, return to the basic principles of natural healthy alignment, practice applying them to specific activities, and make the necessary environmental and prop adjustments so you will not have to strain your voice equipment.

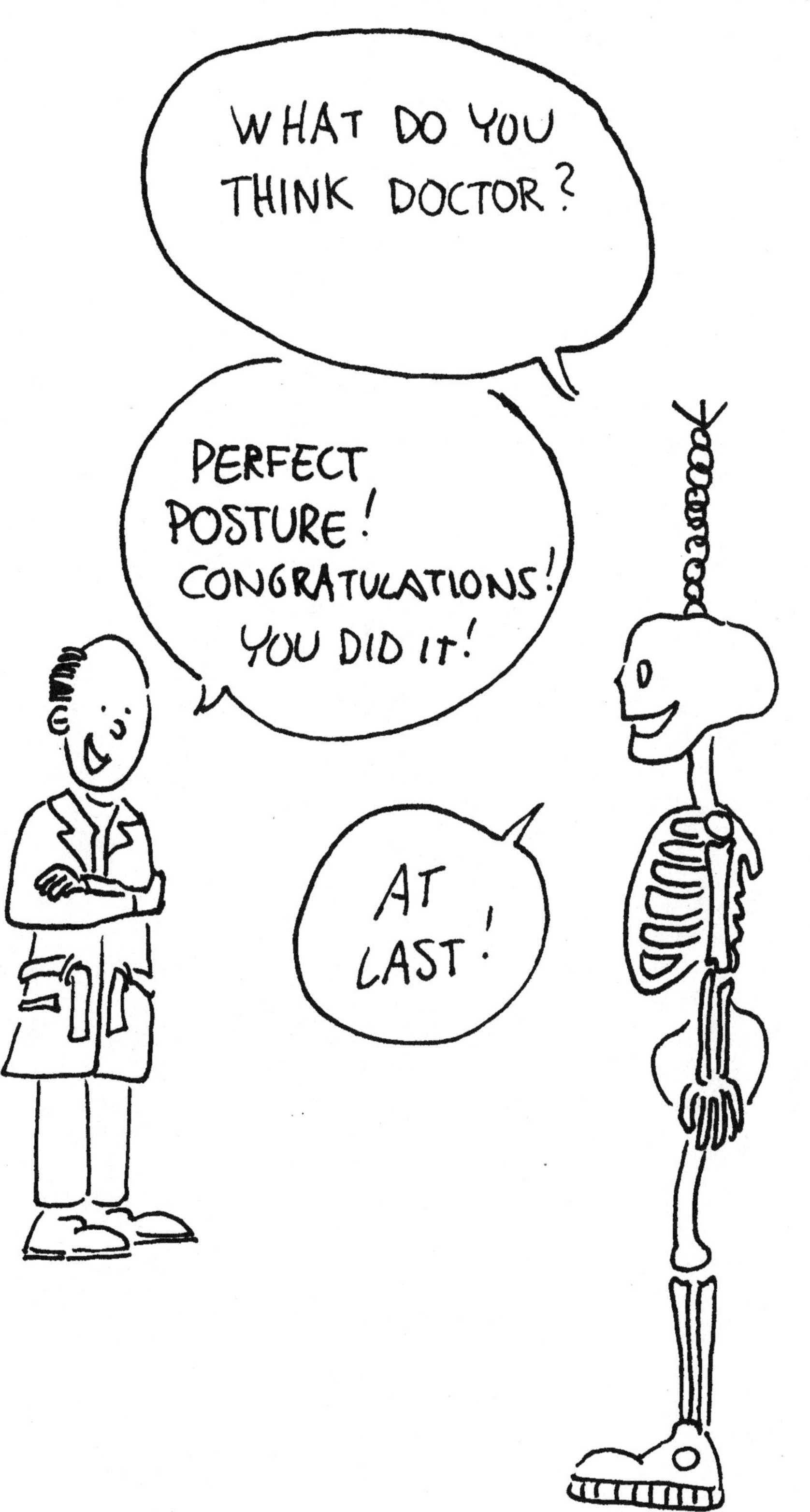
AFTER YEARS OF PRACTISE...
WHAT DO YOU THINK DOCTOR?
PERFECT POSTURE! CONGRATULATIONS! YOU DID IT!
AT LAST!

B. RE-PROGRAM THE SYSTEM:

How will you re-program your body to re-adopt the natural posture you were born with? It's simple: Rehearse, Rehearse, Rehearse!

Plan to review your favourite homo erectus behaviours as frequently as possible every day: ideally no more than 30 minutes of your waking day should pass between rehearsals. Rehearsals will consist of a few simple instructions you give yourself, such as: "let my helium head float freely"; "let my spine lengthen, my back and chest widen"... Choose a set of self-instructions that have had most meaning and dramatic effects for you. (The posters in the appendix may serve as a starting point, but feel free to customize your program.)

Don't forget to use important tools that give you immediate feedback about your body's response to the instructions (mirror; observant friends; body monitors; floor/wall...)! Continue each rehearsal until healthy alignment feels secure (rehearsals will probably be longer in the beginning of your program (maybe 10-15 minutes), much shorter once you become a pro (maybe 2-3 minutes).

Rehearse first thing in the day before you do any talking. Rehearse in the shower, rehearse on your way to work, rehearse while you sit at your desk or stand in front of your class, during your work breaks, before making a phone call...

How will you remember to rehearse? Well, now you can be creative... Engage family, friends, students and colleagues who will *nag* you, or better yet, *rehearse* with you; post some reminder notes in frequently-visited places: on the refrigerator, bathroom mirror, computer, telephone, dashboard ...

C. HABITUALIZE:

If you are rehearsing diligently to re-program your body's alignment, you will be able to apply healthy posture to lots of different activities: standing; sitting; walking; running; playing sports; singing; **talking!** You will find your body slipping into these healthy relationships because they feel good and look good. **It is OK to apply some obsession and vanity to the terrific way good posture looks and feels.**

DOCTOR! I SEEM TO HAVE RECAPSED! I DID PUT REMINDER NOTES ALL OVER THE PLACE JUST LIKE YOU TOLD ME TO. BUT IT DOESN'T SEEM TO HELP! SAY, ISN'T THERE MAYBE AN EASIER WAY TO GO ABOUT THIS POSTURE THING?
LIKE: POP A PILL?
I MEAN, REALLY THIS IS THE 20TH CENTURY!

Physical Program Step 2:

Getting the Vocal Engine Started - Coordinated Voice Onset (CVO)

If you read about the breathing equipment earlier, you've already re-acquainted your body with the natural voice onset apparatus **("hm!").** Once you restore the natural vocal ignition system, you'll be able to use it to support your clearest, most powerful and most flexible vocal tones for speech.

Why do we call it Coordinated Voice Onset or CVO? ... because onset of your speaking voice involves the natural coordination of at least three functions:

1. initiation of breath-flow from the lungs
2. approximation of the two vocal folds
3. resonance in the vocal channels

If you are motivated to speak and your body is alert, relaxed and tuned-in to your motivations, the three functions coordinate themselves automatically. If you've succumbed to the giggles recently, you may remember what CVO feels like when it is unrestrained. You also experience CVO each time you respond automatically with **"hm!"** *(Oh, that's interesting!)* or **"m hm"** *(yes)*

Let's take advantage of your body's familiarity with the CVO to restore and recharge it for speech:

A. EXPLORE AND DISCOVER:

Take turns reading the instructions slowly to each other, while you explore and discover.

The ultimate position for CVO exploration is supine: find a nice spot on the carpeted floor and lie on your back. Take a few minutes to indulge in gravity. Observe a few cycles of breath flow. Notice how air moves in and out of your body like the tide flowing in and out of the sea. Feel how gravity helps release breath out of the body. After the breath-tide flows out, hold it out of the body for a few seconds with your deep abdominal muscles... then release.

After this interruption, feel how the abdomen expands naturally to replace air deep into the body, as the breath-tide rushes in. The muscles you used to hold the breath out include the vocal ignition and power system.

Now instead of holding breath out with the abdominal muscles, allow these muscles to initiate voice onset: wait until the breath-tide flows out of the lungs, so you will be able to feel the response deep in your abdomen... then without hesitation, quickly and *briefly* do a CVO:

"hm!"

Think about the meaning of "hm" *(Oh, that's interesting!)*, so the physical response will be spontaneous and natural, not hesitant and contrived. Don't think about *how* to start sound, just set your body up for a natural reaction.

(It may seem counter-intuitive to start vocal tones at the end of the tidal breath. Be assured that your lungs are still about ***40% full,*** *even at the end of a normal breath, so you're not actually starting sound on an empty tank.)*

Starting your first CVO at about 40% full, repeat this brief vocal response several times. Make sure you allow the abdominal muscles to relax between CVOs, so the breath-tide can flow back in:

"hm!, hm!, hm!, hm!, hm!, hm!, hm!, hm!, hm! ..."

Observe the sensations of CVO. The primary sensation is related to action in the deep abdominal muscles, right?

Notice that breath-replacement between sounds is a natural consequence of stopping the CVO tone: let's call this automatic inward breath-tide **"Respiratory Release" (RR).** During energetic speech, the breathing equipment works like a spring system that compresses and moves air for CVO, then expands the lung cavity automatically for breath-replacement (and to get ready for the next CVO).

The throat plays a very passive role during CVO, since vibration of the vocal folds is automatic once they are in "ready for vocalizing" position. You may notice a brief resonance sensation like a buzzing in your vocal channels as the vibration occurs.

Find a rhythm to repeat CVO that suits your current energy level:

"hm!(RR) hm!(RR) hm!(RR) ...

*(remember: **RR** means "Respiratory Release" that is, the immediate natural release of abdominal muscles, allowing the breath-tide to flow in quickly between sounds).*

Start with a rate of about three repetitions per second. You will know when your repetition rate matches your current adrenalin level, because the CVO system will seem to be self-perpetuating: (and you will not gasp for air after several repetitions). In fact, once you submit your body to the spring-like actions of CVO-RR-CVO-RR, you will feel as though you could continue responding in this way indefinitely, or at least until the cows come home.

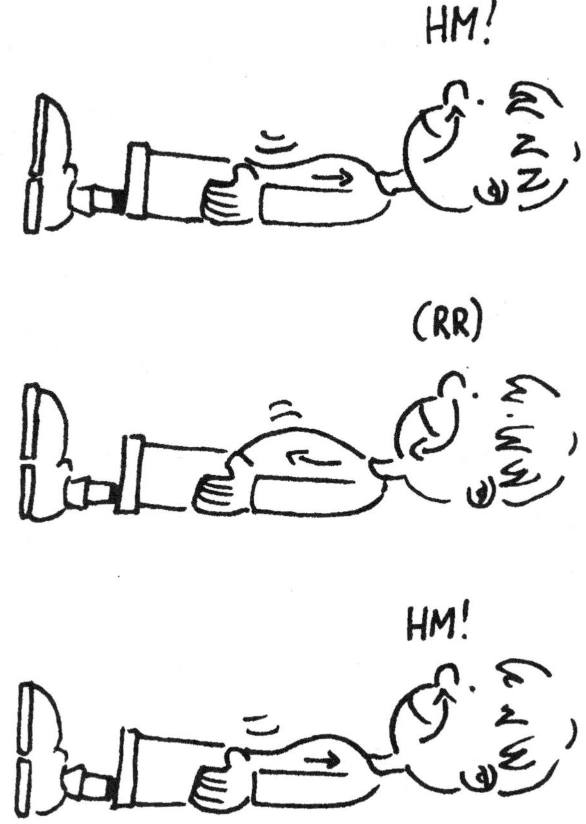

CVO ON YOUR FEET:

The CVO response is equally effective in upright positions: sitting or standing, assuming you apply principles of healthy posture as you vocalize.

Practice CVO while sitting or standing in front of a full-length mirror: Notice the absence of activity in your upper body during CVO (no head, neck, jaw, face or shoulder movements). If you're not wearing lots of bulky clothing, you will be able to see the CVO-RR activity in your abdomen.

You have just rediscovered one of your most important vocal functions. Enjoy and be proud of yourself!

CVO EXTENSION:

Now that you've rediscovered the CVO mechanism, you can explore its relationship to longer sounds. Remember that the fuel for vocal sound is airflow from the lungs. Like a motor vehicle, a continuous flow of fuel requires a constant pressure on the "accelerator pedal". Your abdominal muscles will play the primary role for acceleration.

Begin by charging the vocal system with some short, playful, bouncy CVOs:

hm!(RR) hm!(RR) hm!(RR) ...

Without adjusting the equipment, extend some of the CVOs several seconds, or until you run out of fuel to support the sounds. Don't be afraid to engage the deep abdominal muscles to maintain the vocal tones! Remember, the vocal accelerator (abdominal muscles) should be depressed throughout the sound production:

hm!(RR) hm!(RR) hmmmmm(RR)

hmmmmmmmmmmmmmmmmmm

mmmmmmmmmmmmmmmmm(RR)...

Should I take a big breath first? *You don't have to worry about "taking a deep breath" to prepare for the longer sounds: the RR system takes its cue from the amount of air being used up, and your message intention. Then it refills the lungs a lot, or a little, according to your estimated vocal needs. Make sure your abdominal muscles stay relaxed for RR so they can respond!*

Now, can you imagine each sustained sound is actually a spoken sentence? Once you feel comfortable turning the sound on and sustaining it with abdominal action, try "thinking" speech sentences while you are extending CVO of different lengths.

When you extend your CVO you will have the opportunity to notice more resonance sensations in your vocal channel. We will be exploring this resonance phenomenon further in an upcoming section of the physical program.

CVO WITH YOUR MOUTH OPEN:

The Mouth-Open version of CVO results in a different sound, but is produced exactly the same way in the vocal ignition system.

Start your exploration lying on your back. Allow your face to relax and your jaw to fall open under the influence of gravity. Let your tongue lie relaxed in the floor of your mouth. After the breath-tide flows out, allow CVO to occur quickly and spontaneously from a deep abdominal muscle response: **"huh!"**

Repeat, making sure the automatic respiratory release occurs between sounds:

huh!(RR) huh!(RR) huh!(RR) huh!(RR)...

Keeping your jaw and throat relaxed open, explore sound extension for "huh", by engaging the abdominal accelerator muscles for longer periods:

huh!(RR) huh!(RR) huuuuuh(RR) huuuuuuuuuuuuuh(RR)

The sound should flow out of your mouth freely in direct response to your deep abdominal muscle action.

Each sustained tone is really the basic action for a spoken sentence that length. **("Hm!")**

Try CVO on some other mouth shapes. Pose for the vowel before you start the vocal engine, so there is no movement in your face, mouth or neck as you initiate and sustain the vocal tone:

"ho!(RR) ho!(RR) ho!(RR) hooooooooooooo(RR) ..."

"hee!(RR) hee!(RR) hee!(RR) heeeeeeeeee(RR) ..."

"hoo!(RR) hoo!(RR) hoo-oo-oo-oo-oo-oo(RR) ..."

"hey!(RR) hey!(RR) heeeeeeeeeeeeeeeey(RR) ..."

(the "h" is simply a reminder to start sound with movement of air. It should be very brief, and barely audible. Keep your throat open, and let each vowel be naturally bright and clear)

RECOGNIZING THE BAD:

It is sometimes useful to contrast the good vocal responses to bad habits that you may have adopted. You can experience an "uncoordinated voice onset" if you take a breath in, then hold it back with your throat muscles as you make a sound. This "glottal attack" involves the valving mechanism in the voice box. You will notice a feeling of resistance and closure in your throat as you push to get a sound out. Be on the lookout for this effect if you rely on a speech recognition system, especially if you have to separate each word!

Notice the "klunk" at the beginning of the sound, like a grunt or a cough. Your throat will become tired and strained if you start your speech with such an uncoordinated voice onset! Ask your body monitors to tell you every time you start sound with a "glottal attack". Each time you catch your body using the "hard" attack, rehearse CVO, to show the vocal equipment the "easy" and natural way to start a sound! Try a throat-opening yawn to relax then go back to your basic CVO response: **"hm!(RR) hm!(RR) ..."**

B. RE-PROGRAM THE SYSTEM:

How will you re-program your vocal equipment to respond in the "good" ways rather than the habitual "bad" ways? It's simple: **Rehearse, Rehearse, Rehearse!**

Plan to rehearse your CVO as frequently as possible throughout every day: ideally no more than 30 minutes of your waking day should pass between rehearsals. The rehearsals will consist of preparation for, and multiple repetitions of CVO productions: ***"hm!"*** or ***"huh!"***, or both. Continue each rehearsal until the CVO response feels natural and automatic for "hm" or "huh" (typical rehearsals will last 2-5 minutes).

Rehearse first thing in the day, before you even get out of bed, and prior to any talking. Rehearse in the shower, rehearse on your way to work, rehearse during your work breaks, rehearse before initiating a phone call...

How will these rehearsals change my voice? ... The frequent repetition of this basic vocal action will re-enact it; if the "good" onset action is rehearsed more frequently than "bad" voice onsets, the body will begin to re-adopt the more accessible and natural behaviour, CVO, as its habit.

C. HABITUALIZE:

If you are rehearsing diligently to re-program your body's vocal ignition system, you will become very familiar with the sensations of CVO. You will notice your body using CVO naturally and easily for spontaneous greetings and responses:

"Hi!"(RR) **"Hello?"(RR)** **"Hey!"(RR)**

"M Hm"(RR) **"Sure"(RR)**

"Fine"(RR) **"OK"(RR)** **"Now?"(RR)**

"Really?!"(RR) **"No Way!"(RR) ...**

After practicing CVO extension, you will find your speech can be naturally charged by the abdominal accelerator. With a reliable energy source, your vocal equipment will be more responsive to your feelings and intentions, and reflect them more easily and honestly in your vocal tone. Encourage and enjoy these natural speech functions.

Physical Program Step 3:

Liberating the Speech Resonators and Articulators

Do the following exercises frequently throughout the day, so your speech resonators and articulators are always relaxed and ready for action:

Face-Up to Freedom of Expression:

When the muscles of your face are relaxed, they will allow you to express emotions naturally. On the other hand, if your face is constantly bound up in tension, it may get stuck in certain positions (like the forced social grimace, or the worried look) and talking may feel effortful. Facial tension can also restrict the quality and power of your voice by limiting important movements of the speech articulators.

Practice "face-ups" like you would any other aerobic activity: with attention to detail, and with a commitment to work-out and relax all areas. Use a mirror to help confirm that you are moving only the small area of your face defined in each exercise on the following page.

Notice that some facial postures speak for themselves: what meaning is conveyed by lowering your eyebrows?; raising your eyebrows?; pushing your lower lip down?

FACE-UPS:

Raise your eyebrows... Lower your eyebrows... Raise then lower your eyebrows repeatedly until they feel a bit tired, warm and tingly... Relax your forehead

Open your eyes wide... Close your eyes... Open then close your eyes repeatedly until they feel a bit tired, warm and tingly... Relax your eyes

Squish your nose up toward your eyes... Release it down... Squish your nose up and release it down repeatedly until it feels a bit tired, warm and tingly... Relax your nose

Push your cheeks up toward your eyes... Release them down... Push your cheeks up and release them down repeatedly until they feel a bit tired, warm and tingly... Relax your cheeks

Push your lips forward (like a pucker)... Spread your lips back toward your ears... Push your lips forward and back repeatedly until they feel a bit tired, warm and tingly... Relax your lips

Bite your teeth together lightly... Release the bite... Bite then release repeatedly until your jaw feels a bit tired, warm and tingly... Relax your jaw so it falls off your face

Push your lower lip down toward your chin... Push your lower lip up... Push your lower lip down then up repeatedly until it feels a bit tired, warm and tingly... Relax your lower lip

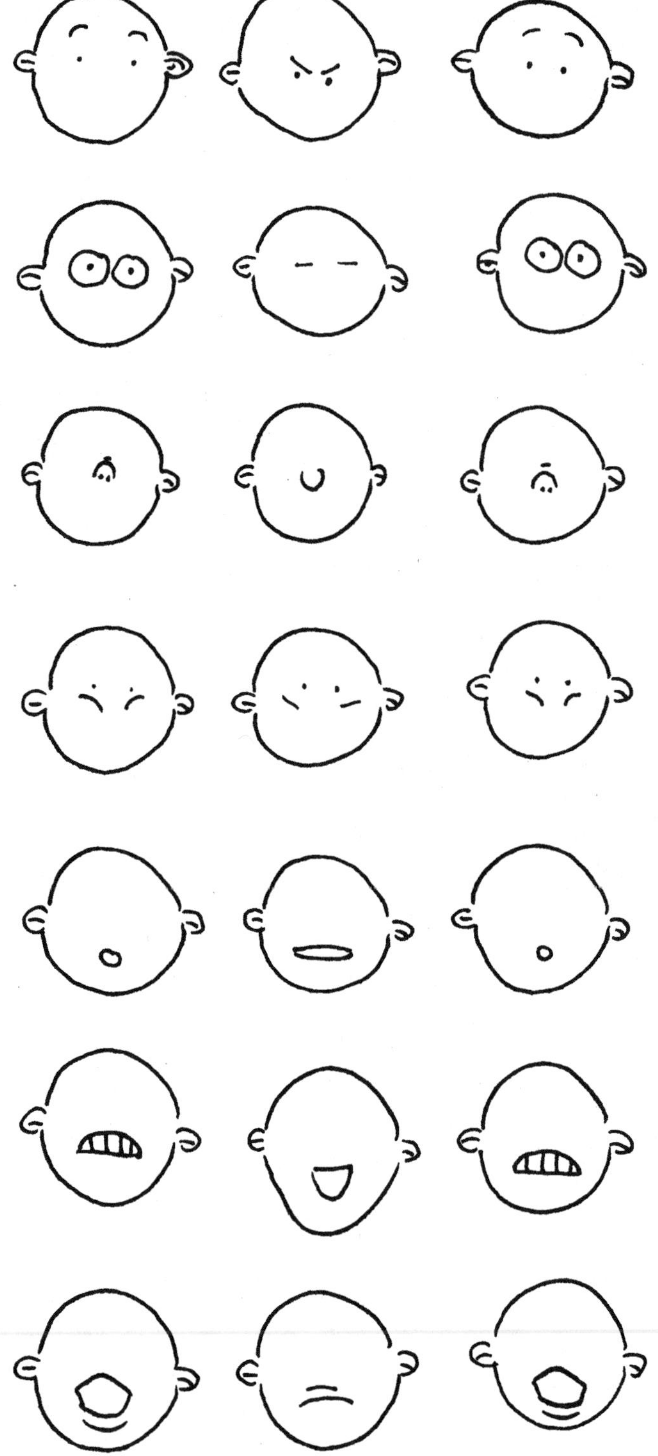

LIBERATE YOUR LIPS:

The lips form one of your important speech articulators. Their freedom to move is influenced by several areas in the face. A static "position" of the lips, in turn, can restrict other speech functions, like jaw movement. If your face gets stuck in the "social smile" position, your lips will be stiff, and your speech nasal and indistinct. We need to banish the "stiff upper lip" to vocalize with ease.

Using your mirror, gently whisper **"O"**. The upper lip should be stretched forward, like a half-open umbrella, your jaw dropped. Allow your body to breathe through the **"O"**, leaving your jaw hanging, and your tongue lying on the floor of your mouth.

To release tension in lip muscles, close them loosely, and blow air between them so they vibrate and flutter in the breeze. See how long you can keep your lips vibrating in the airflow.

Do the following exercise frequently to remind your monitors what free lip movements feel like during speech (use a mirror):

Gently vocalize the sound sequence: **"OO-EE-OO-EE-OO-EE-OO-EE ..."**

OO - EE - OO

Keep your voice flowing through the transition from "oo" to "ee". Make sure your lips pucker forward for "oo" and spread back for "ee". Start with slow repetitions, then increase the rate so you are changing sounds at the rate of normal speech.

Now try a new sound sequence: **"O-AY-O-AY-O-AY-O-AY-O-AY ..."**
(Your lips come forward for "O", and back for "AY")

Many sounds in speech need forward lip movements like the ones you have just practiced ("oo"; "o"; "w"; "r"; "sh"). Notice how your lips want to be liberated when you talk!

EXPAND YOUR THROAT CHANNEL:

When you breathe through an open **"O",** with your jaw relaxed and your tongue lying lazily on the floor of your mouth, your throat channel will begin to open.

You can enhance the open relaxed feeling by initiating a yawn-stretch. As you start a yawn, feel the expansion in your mouth and throat. Think of your upper lip as an umbrella that extends gently out over your top teeth to keep your lower face relaxed and the breath channel open.

Allow your throat to stay open while you are vocalizing. If your jaw tends to open very wide when you yawn, you should read the Jaw Abuse Warning in the next section. Every day is Be-Kind-To-Your-Jaw-Day!

PUT YOUR WALL TO WORK FOR YOU:

Push your chair back against the wall, and lean against the chair back. Drop your head gently back against the wall, and release all your head-weight into the wall. Allow your jaw to fall open (don't exaggerate or force the jaw open!). Let your tongue be a rug in the floor of your mouth. Feel your throat channel opening. Enjoy the sensation of air flowing easily and quietly through the open mouth and throat channels (don't exaggerate the breath-size: just observe the way your body wants to breathe now). This is the easy way air should flow into your body when you are speaking.

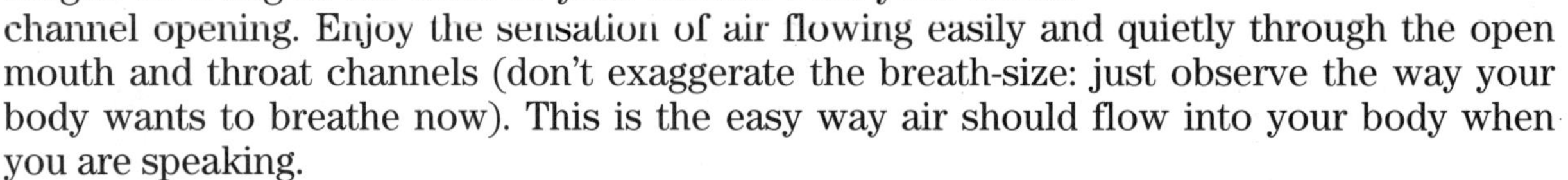

The Jaw Bone is NOT Connected to the ...

The jaw is an independent bone that is suspended from the skull and neck by muscles and ligaments. Because of these attachments, jaw movements can be restricted by tension in the face, neck, tongue and throat. Therefore, prerequisites to a relaxed and mobile jaw articulator include healthy posture and relaxed facial muscles. If the jaw is restricted during speech, it can transmit its tension to muscles of the throat, tongue and voicebox: YIKES!

If you tend to clench your jaw or grind your teeth, or hold your lower face in a social smile posture, you are probably experiencing some speech and vocal limitations, and facial discomfort as a result.

The jaw is capable of several types of movements. When we eat, it may move forward and back, up and down, and side to side. **When we use the jaw for talking or singing, the main movement is a down and up movement, with the jaw pivoting within its joints, like a door pivoting on its hinges.**

The jaw joint is located directly in front of the ear hole. Place your fingers flat on the sides of your face to feel the area over the jaw joint. It will become evident if you gently push your jaw forward a few millimetres: your fingers will feel a slight bulging over the joint. This bulge should not be evident when you are talking. Instead, your face should stay flat when your jaw is moving for speech.

GRAVITY AND THE JAW:

Let's experiment with the passive opening of the jaw that forms the basis for speech movements.

Start in supine position (lying on your back) or reclined in a chair with your head resting back against a head-rest or the wall. Allow your face to relax under the influence of gravity, and let your jaw fall away from the face naturally. Do not force the jaw to open with your face muscles, simply let it drop down and back as your face muscles relax. Let the tongue drop with the jaw, as if it is a rug on the floor of your mouth. Allow the air to flow through your naturally open mouth and throat. With your hand, push your jaw closed, then let it fall away from the face again. Feel the weight of the jaw bone!

Recreate the jaw release in sitting and standing positions. Remember to keep your head floating free above the neck, then let the jaw fall down off the face of its own weight. After the jaw drops, push it closed with your hand, then let it fall down again. Notice a passive jaw drop does not reflect the biggest opening your jaw can make: to open the jaw maximally you must use face muscles ... don't do that!

THE HAND-COMMAND:

Wiggle your jaw gently up and down with your hand, keeping all your face muscles relaxed. Notice how the jaw wants to pivot down and back as it is opened passively. Do not try to make the largest jaw movement possible: just allow a loose and passive movement that only your hand commands. Keep the upper lip relaxed like a half-opened umbrella over the top teeth.

If you plaster a tense smile on your face your jaw will lock in place. Let's prove it: apply your most insincere smile and then try to wiggle your jaw gently in its passive, pivotal open-close action: stuck, right!

CLAM-UP!:

If you find your jaw is very stubborn and resistant, you may want to start with an isometric exercise: to contrast a tense jaw with a relaxed jaw, alternately clench your teeth, then relax the jaw. After several repetitions of jaw isometrics, see if you can leave the jaw hanging open and relaxed, and let the air flow in through your open mouth and throat. Push your jaw closed with your hand, then let it drop open again. Do not try to exaggerate the width of jaw opening: freedom NOT extent of jaw movements determines easy, natural speech!

Warning! Be Gentle: "Every Day is Be-Kind-to-Your-Jaw Day"!

The Jaw is a rather delicate joint. If you abuse and misuse it by clenching, grinding and pushing it to its limits, you will experience discomfort, movement restrictions and, ultimately, deterioration of the joint. The gentle passive jaw movements that gravity dictates provide a model for jaw kindness. Avoid movements that cause strain, clicking, pain and effort. Do not test the jaw by pushing it forward, down or sideways in exaggerated movements: this is jaw cruelty!

When you open your mouth very wide to take a big bite of a sandwich, apple ... or to indulge in a big yawn, you may strain the jaw joint. Don't take chances: cut your food into manageable pieces, and protect your jaw when you yawn:

To protect your jaw when you enjoy a yawn:

Hold your jaw bone at the front firmly with your hand. As you yawn, guide your jaw gently back and down as your mouth opens, so the opening is gradual, gentle and pivotal, like the passive jaw release. Enjoy the stretch in your throat, lips and tongue without pushing the jaw to its limits!

... and Now for a Good Jaw-Wag!

The jaw movements that occur during speech to articulate and resonate vocal sounds are simple, small and loose. They should be the same type of movements you created with your hand pivoting your jaw open and closed.

A. EXPLORE AND DISCOVER:

You can feel the constant loose jaw movements during a simple syllable repetition.

Pretend you are learning some new languages that have only two sounds: a consonant and a vowel. Using a mirror for visual confirmation, practice your new languages with your jaw dropping for each vowel, then being lifted upward to create the consonant.

Imagine you are a marionette-puppet, with only a heavy wooden jaw and a string to articulate with. Keep your tongue absolutely still on the floor of the mouth: remember marionettes don't have tongues!

Keep the upper lip in neutral half-open umbrella position. The jaw starts in "mouth-open for breathing and vocalizing position":

NEW LANGUAGES:

1. PLUTONIAN: AnAnAnAnAnAnAnAnAnAnAnAnAnAnA....

↓ ↓ ↓ ↓ ↓ ↓ ↓ ↓ ↓ ↓ ↓ ↓ ↓ ↓ ↓

(say the "A" vowel like "ah"; the arrows mean your jaw drops for each new "ah")
(use your regular speech speed, or about 4 syllables/second)
(don't cheat by articulating "n" with your tongue tip: you will create "n" automatically when the jaw carries your tongue-mass to the roof of your mouth!)

2. VENUTIAN:

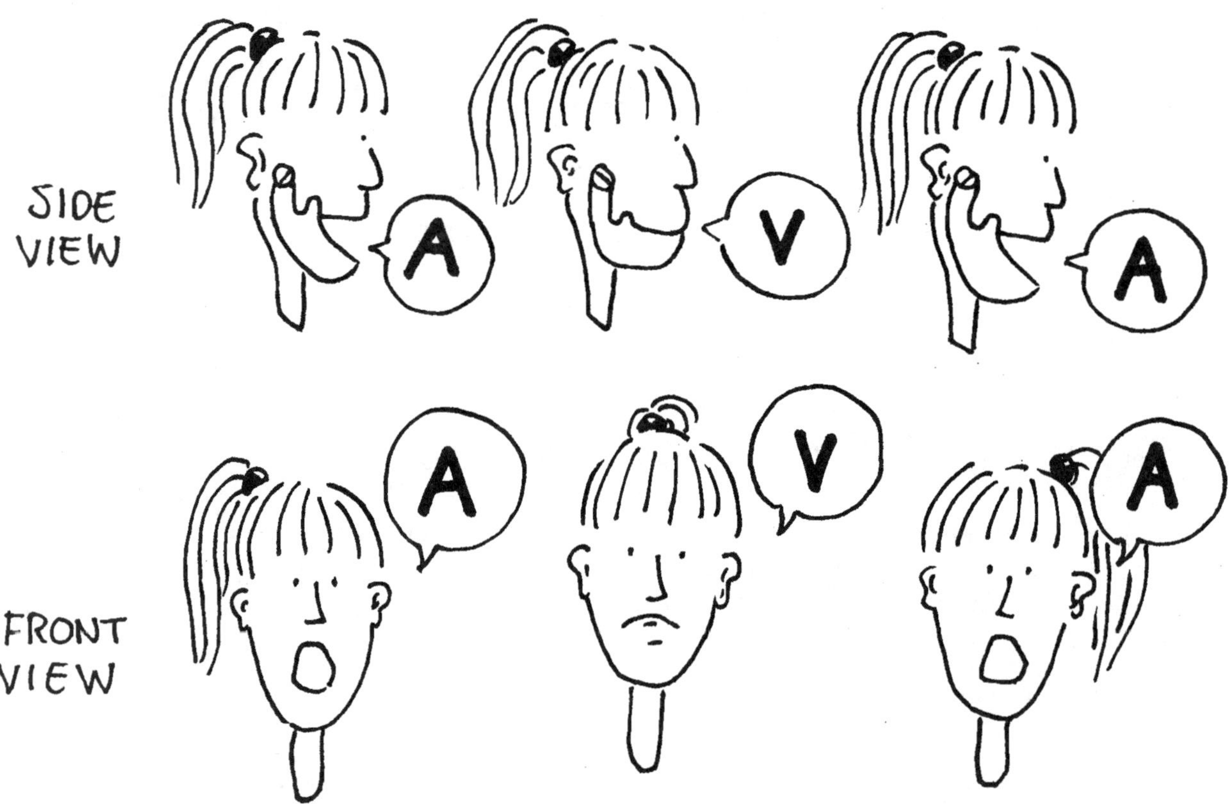

(let gravity be responsible for the jaw drop on each "ah")
(don't cheat by articulating "v" with lower-lip movement: you will create "v" automatically when the jaw carries your lower lip up to your upper teeth!)

3. MARTIAN: AdAdAdAdAdAdAdAdAdAdAdAdAdAdAd...

↓ ↓ ↓ ↓ ↓ ↓ ↓ ↓ ↓ ↓ ↓ ↓ ↓ ↓ ↓

4. URANIAN: AsAsAsAsAsAsAsAsAsAsAsAsAsAsAsAs...

↓ ↓ ↓ ↓ ↓ ↓ ↓ ↓ ↓ ↓ ↓ ↓ ↓ ↓ ↓ ↓

5. MAKE UP YOUR OWN LANGUAGE WITH A CONSONANT AND A VOWEL

Try some syllables with different vowels. Keep your tongue slack, and your consonants very casual: let the jaw do all the articulating for now ... Pretend you are saying something important; use your regular speech speed and normal inflection patterns, not a monotone:

You will probably find it feels more natural to drop the jaw for "open" vowels, like "ah", "o" and "ay", than for "close" vowels like "ee" and "oo". The jaw should drop for *all* vowels so that they can resonate properly. Use an easy model like: "AHnAHnAH..." to show your jaw how to drop for "ee" and "oo".

You can use the loose free jaw wag of simpler languages: Martian, Plutonian, Uranian, Venutian to apply to your own language now. Start with a simple jaw-wag model in front of the mirror:

AHnAHnAHnAHnAH... ↓ ↓ ↓ ↓ ↓ using the same loose wags, convert to a simple speech task like counting:

AHnAHnAH, One, Two, Three, Four, Five ... ↓ ↓ ↓ ↓ ↓

Each of these words has one syllable, so the jaw should drop passively for the vowel of each word! Remember to use natural inflection and your regular speech speed, or a normal speed of four to six syllables per second.

If you are a motor-mouth, remember the following rule:

Motor-Mouth Rule: The faster you talk; that is, the more syllables you say in a second, minute or hour; the looser your jaw needs to be to do its job properly! If you are a motor-mouth, loosen up and slow down! Learn about phrasing and prolongation.

You have now rediscovered your model for healthy, relaxed jaw movements during speech. Congratulations!

B. RE-PROGRAM THE SYSTEM:

As with healthy posture and CVOs, re-programming your speech equipment to function with a naturally loose face and jaw requires frequent rehearsals.

Plan to rehearse your marionette-jaw as frequently as possible: ideally no more than 30 minutes of your waking day should pass between rehearsals. The rehearsals will consist of face-ups, lip-liberation, throat-expansion and jaw-release, followed by multiple repetitions of jaw-wags, starting with the easiest sounds. Continue each rehearsal until the jaw-wag response feels natural and automatic. Use a mirror frequently to confirm that your *jaw* is wagging freely, not just your *lower lip or tongue.*

Rehearse first thing in the day, before you even get out of bed, and prior to any talking. Rehearse in the shower, rehearse on your way to work, rehearse during your work breaks, rehearse before initiating a phone call... *How will you remember to rehearse? Post some reminder notes about jaw-wags along with your other vocal warm-up activities: posture; CVO; face-ups... in frequently-visited places: on the refrigerator, in the bathroom, on your computer, telephone, dashboard ...*

How will these rehearsals change my voice? The frequent repetition of a basic jaw-wag action will make it become familiar to the body; in fact if the "good" jaw-wag action is practiced more frequently than the stiff upper lip or jaw-clench, the body will undoubtedly begin to adopt this more accessible, natural behaviour as its habit.

C. HABITUALIZE:

If you are rehearsing diligently to liberate your jaw, you will become familiar with the sensations of jaw-wag during speech. You will find your body using jaw-wag after rehearsals for as long as you stay attentive to it.

Once you are confident about jaw-wag in rehearsal sets with the basic syllable repetitions, and word series like counting, try some more creative language like nursery rhymes or memorized passages. Use your mirror to confirm constant loose jaw-wags, and to observe the naturalness of a relaxed and mobile jaw during speech.

Talk yourself into rehearsing some sentences, with marionette jaw, that you might say frequently. Allow creativity to flow, and tell yourself some good stories in the mirror, with your jaw wagging. Invite family and friends to observe, listen, and participate in some jaw-wagging activities. You might want to start with some simple monologues:

- **Recite a poem, words to a song, or a pledge you have memorized.**
- **Describe a procedure you know well, such as changing a tire, getting to school or work, baking biscuits...**

(Remember to keep your sensors "tuned-in" to constant loose jaw-wags! Let gravity do its job on your heavy jaw bone)

Once you are confident about jaw-wags for monologues, you can engage your family and friends to rehearse during conversations. Make sure you stop frequently to evaluate your jaw performance!

P.S. Untie your Tongue!

The tongue is a set of muscle fibres that run in many different directions. It is actually a much larger and deeper set of muscles than you normally see in a mirror, since it extends down into the jaw bone, and back deep into your throat. The tongue is linked by muscles to the jaw, throat, palate, neck and voicebox. When it is not held in tense postures, the tongue is capable of a large repertoire of acrobatic maneuvers, including movements that create speech sounds on the outward flowing vocal tone.

GRAVITY AND THE TONGUE:

In its rest position, when we are not talking, singing, eating or doing other acrobatic maneuvers with the tongue, it should lie flat on the floor of the mouth, like a rug. Gravity helps the tongue assume the rug position on the mouth's floor.

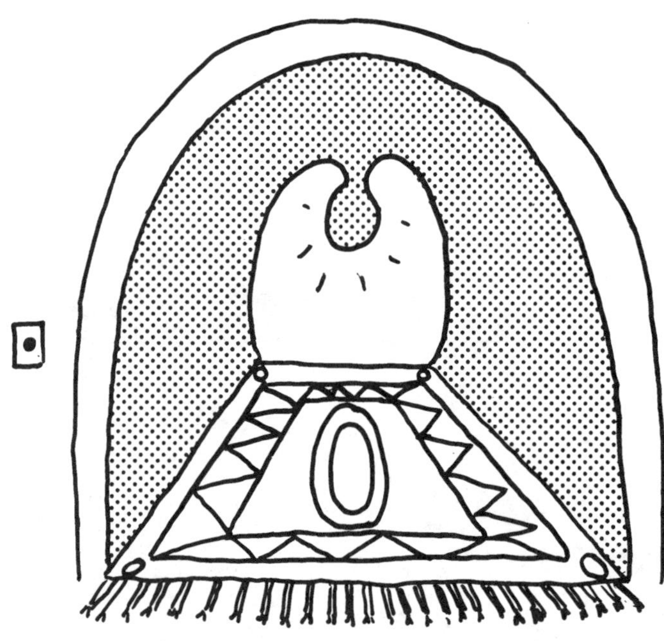

THE TONGUE ASSUMES THE RUG POSITION

Let your jaw fall free under the influence of gravity. The tongue falls down with the jaw. Let your tongue rest lazily on the floor of your mouth, so it touches the back edges of all your bottom teeth. Enjoy breathing through your relaxed open mouth and throat: feel the air flowing freely over the lazy tongue. If your tongue starts to feel too long and wide for your mouth cavity, let it slide forward and rest on your bottom teeth and lips as you enjoy breathing through your open mouth and throat.

This indulgence in relaxation may bring on some yawns. Enjoy them, but protect your jaw from opening too wide! Then let your tongue return to its relaxed rug-like position on the floor of your mouth, resting against your lower teeth...

Sometimes the tongue gets tense and shy, and pulls backwards into the throat cavity. At other times, it may feel aggressive and force itself forward against the teeth; or defy gravity and push against the roof of the mouth. The result of all these tongue postures is bad for your voice: TENSION! The tension will affect all areas connected to the tongue: jaw, throat, palate, voicebox!

When you are not talking, tune in your monitors to spy on your tongue. You can sneak up on the tongue by peeking into a mirror as your jaw drops:

- Is your tongue a rug? ... or is it retreating into your throat, pushing up, or forward...

- Can you see signs of teeth prints on the edges of your tongue? (this is an indication that your tongue was taking on an aggressive posture, pushing itself against the teeth, not resting passively on the floor of your mouth)

- Is your tongue-rug smooth and flat, or does it show signs of over-use: waves, wrinkles, bumps, dimples, grooves, jitters? As the breath flows through your open relaxed mouth, see if you can calm your tongue.

A SPECIAL TONGUE MONITOR: Our bodies are equipped with an excellent monitoring device that can help us detect tongue and jaw tension: **The Thumb!**

One of the main highways for Tongue-Jaw (TJ) muscle fibres runs from the tip of the tongue and the front of the jaw to the top of your neck. You can find this highway with your thumb if you run it along the base of the front of your jaw bone, moving it backwards toward the neck. Stop in the middle of the bottom of your face and press your thumb upward.

Warning: do not adopt the Jaw Jut posture to conduct this investigation: keep your chin level and parallel to the floor!

Try to find a soft hollow space with your thumb, to indicate that your TJ muscles are relaxed. If the area feels hard and resistant, check for tense postures in your neck, jaw, and lower face. (Shake your head gently in the "No" movement; release your jaw to gravity; breathe through your mouth). Now, swallow intentionally to feel the TJ muscles tighten and push against your thumb. This muscle activity is normal during a swallow, but is not appropriate during speech!

Let the tongue be a rug, and feel how the muscles soften under your chin so your thumb slides up into the hollow behind your jaw bone. Keep these muscles passive as the air flows in and out through your open mouth and throat.

TJs and CVOs:

This is an excellent time to return to CVOs:

With your thumb monitor stationed at its post under the chin, review the basic CVO production:

"hm!" (tongue is a rug, lips are lightly closed)

"huh!" (tongue is a rug, lips parted, jaw hanging)

Your thumb monitor should be reporting no action in the TJ muscles before, during, or after CVO (unless you swallow)

Try CVO repetition to reinforce inactivity of TJ muscles during vocal sound ignition and RR:

hm!(RR) hm!(RR) hm!(RR)... (keep TJ muscles passive!)

huh!(RR) huh!(RR) huh!(RR)... (let your jaw hang loose!)

(If your thumb monitor detects some activity in TJ muscles, focus on a slack tongue, head release, jaw release, and breath support from deep within the abdominal cavity: Remember do not prepare for CVO with a deep breath in! Start CVO at the bottom of the breath, where you can feel the deep abdominal ignition system.)

With the help of your thumb monitor, rehearse some sound extensions to confirm the TJ muscles do not have to help keep the vocal engine running. Feed the sound from your breath energy centre, not your throat!

hm!(RR) hm!(RR) hmmmmmmmmmmmmmmmm...

huh!(RR) huh!(RR) huuuuuuuuuuuuuuuuuuuh...

Experiment with other vowel shapes and CVO while your thumb reminds the TJ muscles to stay passive. You will notice the surface of your tongue can do its sound-shaping work without any assistance from the deeper TJ muscles. This leaves the throat and voice-box free of any TJ holds during speech. (Remember to keep your face muscles free and alive, and your jaw passive! The jaw is in gravity-dropped position for all vowels...)

As you speak or sing, you should feel minimal, if any TJ activity. The constant free jaw wag is the best protection against TJ invasion into your speech.

MORE TONGUE RELAXATION AND AEROBICS:

Do these exercises frequently to release tension at the root of the tongue, and to free your whole tongue for easy articulation.

1) Let your thumb go on duty as TJ monitor. Slowly release your tongue forward along the floor of your mouth, over the bottom teeth and lip, until it is hanging relaxed and wide over your chin like a rug hanging over a window sill. Let your jaw pivot gently down and back to accommodate the tongue release. It should take at least 20 seconds to release your tongue all the way. Do not allow the TJ muscles to tighten: this indicates you are pushing your tongue, rather than releasing it forward.

" HANGING OUT THE RUG "

2) Bring out your mirror to help monitor this acrobatic trick: With your hand, release your jaw down and back to its passive open position, and hold it there firmly. Imagine you are going to glue the tip of your tongue-rug to the backs of your bottom teeth. Roll it under and stick the top of your tongue tip there with your imaginary glue. Release the back and deep root of your tongue and roll it gently forward as far as it will go, like a wheel (or a rug being rolled and unrolled). Allow the tongue to stay flat and smooth like a rug as it rolls forward. Feel the gentle stretch at the base of the tongue. Keep the tip of your tongue stuck to the bottom teeth. Roll the tongue rug back and forth, back and forth:

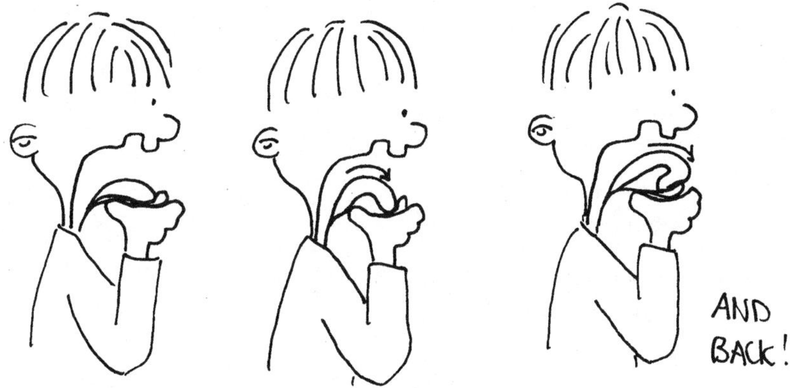

Now put a vocal tone behind this tongue aerobic:

"HuhYuhYuhYuhYuhYuh..."

Let the tongue do all the work. *(Keep your jaw still and passive! Your vocal tone should flow freely through your open throat and mouth as you free the base of your tongue-rug by rolling it.)*

Physical Program Step 4:

Tuning the Resonators and Getting the Buzz on Speech

Resonance refers to enhancement of a sound wave, like your vocal tone vibrations. The exact resonance properties are determined by the size, shape and texture of cavities that a sound passes through. You can hear the effects of resonance, and you can also feel them. By hearing and feeling the resonance buzz in speech, you can feed the vocal vibrations and tune them to your liking.

A. EXPLORE AND DISCOVER:

To prepare for getting the buzz on speech, make sure your body is aligned naturally, your jaw and tongue are passive, and your throat channel is "open".

Let's explore vocal resonance sensations on nasal sounds first.

Start with your jaw hanging, and your upper lip-umbrella closed loosely over your lower lip, so the sound goes through your nose: As always, you should initiate sound with a CVO; then extend the hum by continuing to feed energy into the resonators from your abdominal accelerator (don't be afraid to squeeze the abdomen gently with your muscles to keep breath-energy flowing):

hm!(RR) hm!(RR) hmmmmmmmmmmmmmmmmmmmmmmmmm...

Tune into your resonance monitors. Where do you feel the buzz?:

LIPS? NOSE? TEETH? HEAD? THROAT? PALATE? CHEST? ELSEWHERE?
(every answer is correct)

To enhance your resonance monitor, place your fingers in strategic locations on your nose, face, forehead, neck, lips ... Feel the resonance energy as it is transmitted from your resonators to your hands. See if the sound energy will expand into different resonance regions under your fingers.

hm!(RR) hm!(RR) hmmmmmmmmmmmmmmmmmmmmmmmmmmmmm...

By feeling the resonance buzz, you can actually increase it. Notice the connection between your flow activation system deep in the abdomen and your resonance sensors, as you let the buzzing sensations grow.

Monitor your TJ muscles under your chin, with your thumb, and make sure they stay soft during the hum-buzz. The stronger the buzz, the more relaxed your TJ muscles will be!

You can explore your nasal resonators on two other sounds:

hn!(RR) hn!(RR) hnnnnnnnnnnnnnnnnnnnnnnnnnnnnnnnn... *
**(plunge into your gut when you need more fuel!)*

hng!(RR) hng!(RR) hngngngngngngngngngngngngngngngng...
(the sound at the end of "ring" and "sing")

HANG THE HUM-BUZZ!

You may find it helpful to explore the buzz from several different body positions:

- head dropped forward toward your chest: **"hmmmmmmmmmmmmm..."**
"hnnnnnnnnnnnn..."

- head dropped back, jaw hanging open: **"hnnnnnnnnnn..."**
"hngngngngngng..."

- whole body dropped forward from the hips: **"hmmmmmmmmmmmmm..."**

- body upright, head nodding loosely side to side, like "NO":

"hmmmmmmmmmmm..."; "hnnnnnnnnnn..."; "hngngngngngng..."

EXTEND THE BUZZ:

Once you discover the nasal buzz, you can extend resonance buzz into other vocal sounds within words.

Start with some words and phrases that are loaded with nasals: "m"; "n"; "ng" Prolong the vocal sounds, so you feel the buzz extending from the nasals into vowels. Make sure your jaw drops open for the vowels: they need resonance space in the mouth!

"Man": Mmmmmmmmmmaaaaaaaaaannnnn

"Mine": Mmmmmmmmmmiiiiiiiiinnnnn

"Many": Mmmmmmmmaaaaaaannnnnnyyyyyy

"Nine": Nnnnnnniiiiiiiiinnnn *(final "e" is silent)*

"Name": Nnnnnnnaaaaaaaaammmmmmm

"Money": Mmmmmmmmmoooooonnnnnnnnneeeeeeee!

Think about lifting the sound energy into the vowels, by keeping the breath-energy flowing. Let the pitch rise slightly on each vowel, and be careful not to let the energy drop too low at the end of a word or phrase... Keep the buzz going to the very end!

Now, you can combine some words in phrases, to experience buzz during speech. Prolong the nasal and vowel segments slightly to give your sensors time to recognize and encourage the buzz:

"More money": MmmmoooooorrrMmmmmoooonnnnneeeeee!
"My name": MmmmyyyyyyNnnnnaaaaaammmm ...
"Nearly noon": NnnnneeeeerrrrllllyyyNnnnoooonnnn
"Never on Monday": NnnneeeeevrrrrrOoooonnnnMmmmooonnnnnndaaaaay
"Make me a millionaire!" (prolong the nasals and vowels)
"Name nine more animals." (prolong the nasals and vowels)

(Notice certain consonants behave like nasals and vowels, and achieve their own buzz-power: r; l; y)

See if you can "think" prolongation, but use a regular speech pattern, and still maintain the buzz through all your vocal sounds in speech. It will feel like a constant invigorating low-voltage electrical energy is living in your mouth, throat or face while you speak. Feeding the buzz provides a stimulating and completely legitimate shortcut to good vocal projection!

More Buzz on Vowels:

As you have already discovered, many speech sounds have resonance energy and buzz. Since VOWELS are naturally the most powerful speech sounds, they have the greatest potential for resonance energy and VOCAL PROJECTION. This works out well, since vowels are also the speech segments that last the longest. Resonant vowels means resonant speech!

As with our nasal buzzers, all that is required to achieve natural vowel resonance is an open, relaxed vocal channel, and continuous breath-flow energy feeding sound into the resonators. If these basic requirements are met, the amount of resonance buzz you feel will reflect the amount of energy coming from the abdominal activator at the same time.

To meet the open vocal channel requirements, use a chair and a wall: place the chair back against the wall; sitting back against the chair, drop your head back and give your head-weight to the wall. Your jaw falls open with gravity, right?! Your tongue is a heavy, wet rug! Let your upper lip umbrella stretch down to half-open position over your top teeth (like a relaxed "O"). Using CVO, initiate and sustain the sound vibration from the deep abdominal activator:

"hO!(RR) hOOOOOOOOOOOO..."
(keep your throat Open!)

Tune in to your resonance sensors. Where do you feel the buzz?:

MOUTH? PALATE? SINUSES? HEAD? LIPS? THROAT? CHEST?
(every answer is correct)

Buzz on "O" several times, and let the resonance energy expand:

"hO!(RR) hOOOOOOOOOOOOOOOOOOOOOOOOOOOOO..."

Now try extending some other vowels. Always start with CVO:

"hOO!(RR) hOO-OO-OO-OO..." *(lip-umbrella 2/3 closed)*

"hEE!(RR) hEEEEEEEEEE..." *(tongue rolls forward like rug-roll; lip-umbrella 1/2 open)*

"hAY!(RR) hAY-AY-AY..." *(tongue forward, jaw dropped)*

"hAh!(RR) hAAAAAAAAAh..." *(all face and mouth parts succumb to gravity)*

Each vowel has its own resonance characteristics and sensations. Let each sound grow in your throat and mouth resonators as you feed them from the abominal activator.

Explore the vowel resonances in a variety of body positions: lying down; head dropped forward; body dropped forward; body upright; head gently nodding "NO".

USE A MOUTH PROP:

To facilitate a relaxed open mouth cavity for vowel resonance, you can use a prop while exploring the buzz:

Prop a slice of round cork between your upper and lower front molars. Without biting hard against the prop, let your jaw drop naturally down and back, and let your tongue be a rug (don't park your tongue in the back of your mouth!) Try the vowel buzzes again with this helper-prop. Do you feel/hear more power as the sounds pass through a bigger resonance cavity?

Vowels form the Resonance River!

You already know how to drop the jaw passively for syllable repetitions: Review the jaw-wag for several primitive languages:

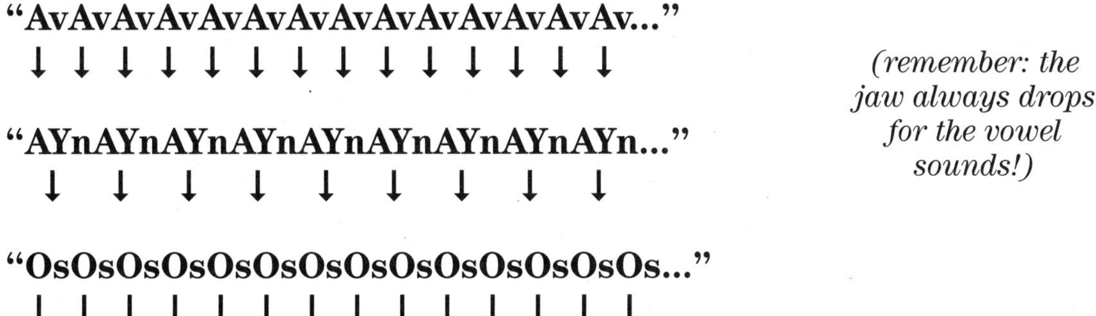

(remember: the jaw always drops for the vowel sounds!)

The vowel sounds form a river of vibrations as they buzz and flow through the open channel in a speech phrase. The resonance current can be felt throughout speech when all the equipment is coordinated, free and energetic. The brief consonant productions "decorate" the vowels, but do not stop the flow of the resonance river.

Review your jaw-wag for connected speech. Combine your jaw-wag skills and vowel resonance enhancement to experience naturally energetic, and EASY fluid speech. *Yeah!*

B. RE-PROGRAM THE SYSTEM:

How will you re-program your speech resonators to "tune-in" and "tune-up"? It's simple: Rehearse, Rehearse, Rehearse! Plan to rehearse your hum-buzz and vowel-buzz as frequently as possible throughout every day, as part of your regular vocal warm-up.

The frequent repetition of natural resonance power will make it become familiar and accessible to the body.

C. HABITUALIZE:

If you are rehearsing diligently to tune into your body's vocal resonance responses, you will become aware of the delightful sensations of speaking with resonance. You will find your body craving the self-stimulation of the resonance buzz. By "tuning-in" to the resonance energy, you will begin to adopt it as a natural phenomenon during speech.

Physical Program Step 5:

Reflections on Inflections - Extending Your Dynamic Pitch Range

The human voice is remarkably flexible when it is free. A free vocal system that is linked to an honest intent results in energetic speech that rises and falls in pitch to enhance the meaning of your message ('inflections'). On the other hand, suppressing emotion during speech results in a tense, monotone speech pattern that reveals little of your true self. Honest lively inflection can make you feel more sincere and energetic.

> As a vibrator, your vocal system is probably capable of creating two or three octaves of pitches (around 24 musical notes!). Special vocal games can help free your vocal equipment so you can discover your full potential for pitches and inflections.

Use the following games as physical therapy to activate steady air-flow for vocalizing, and to stretch and tone your pitch muscles. Include them in your vocal warm-up routine:

Bubbling and Trilling:

The air flowing from your lungs can set the lips into vibration in much the same way it sets the vocal folds into vibration. The same prerequisites apply for sustained lip vibration and vocal fold vibration:

1 - the vibrators need to be loosely touching
2 - the flow needs to be adequate to start the vibration
3 - the flow needs to continue as long as the vibration is required

Press your upper and lower lips together lightly (like for "p"). Keeping them together, blow air between your lips, so you get a "raspberry bubble". (Don't despair if at first this seems impossible. There will be other options for you if the bubble doesn't emerge).

Now turn your vocal motor on lightly during your raspberry-bubble:

"pbrbrbrbrbrbrbrbr..."

(remember to keep your lips together and your breath-flow steady: use your abdominal muscles to activate and sustain the flow; stop for a refill when you run out of air)

Once you can sustain the lip bubble, slide the pitch of your voice down and up during the raspberry bubble. Keep the vocal tone light and playful. Start with small pitch changes, then gradually sweep wider and wider: down gradually, then up gradually.

Do not strain to make the widest pitch range possible. You will probably find the easy range expands with time. Keep your throat and mouth relaxed and keep your lips connected to your flow-activator! Does your vocal-lip bubble remind you of a small truck motor?

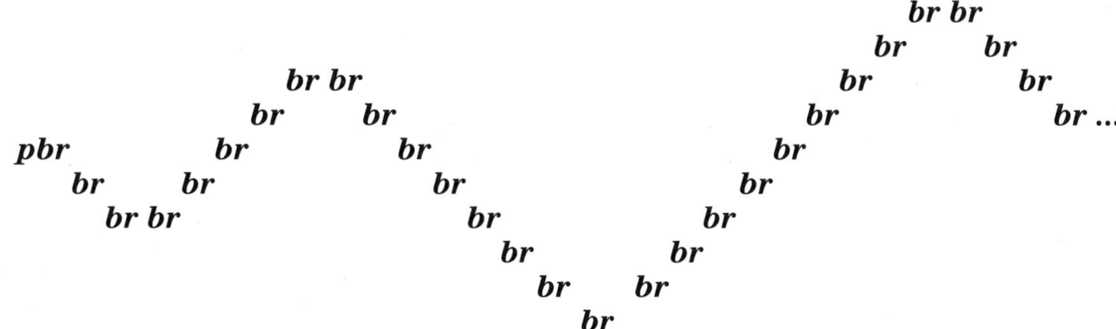

A TRILLING EXPERIENCE:

You may prefer to play with pitch using your tongue as a triller.

Place your tongue tip on the ridge behind your upper teeth (like for "t"). Keeping your tongue in place, blow air over it so it flutters against the roof of your mouth.

Turn on your vocal motor too, but keep it light:

"tdrdrdrdrdrdrdrdrdrdr..." (keep the air flowing!)

Once you can sustain this trilling experience, let your vocal pitch slide down and up, gradually increasing the range. Keep your mouth and throat relaxed and let the airflow do the work!

dr dr
dr dr
dr dr...
dr dr dr
dr dr dr
tdr dr dr dr
dr dr dr dr *Does your tongue trill remind you*
dr dr dr dr *of a small electric drill?*
dr dr

(Remember: don't strain to achieve a particular pitch, just go with the flow, and explore playfully!)

Buzzing on the Finger, Lips and Tongue:

You've probably never buzzed your finger, right?! Vocalizing on your finger gives you the opportunity to monitor a steady airflow and keep your throat relaxed, while you are making a fun sound.

BUZZING ON THE FINGER

Start with your lips in the "OO" position: that is forward and round like a loose pucker, upper lip umbrella 2/3 closed. Place your pointing finger sideways on the lips so it touches your lip "OO". Turn on the vocal motor lightly so you create not only the vowel "OO", but also a distinct buzzing sound as the air and vibrations hit your finger. Keep the "OO" and the finger buzz going together as long as your breath lasts. Keep your abdominal muscles engaged to provide the fuel:

"whoo-oo-oo-oo-oo-oo..."

Once you feel the finger buzz and can keep it steady, let the pitch slide slowly down, then up, with gradually wider pitch sweeps. Keep the tone light and playful. Don't push your voice to the extreme range unless it is comfortable and relaxed!

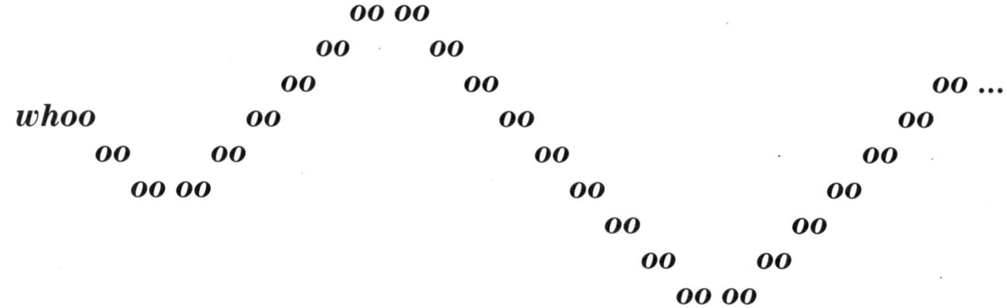

Does your finger-buzz remind you of a kazoo?

Your lips, teeth and tongue can also provide the tools for monitoring constant airflow while you vocalize lightly and explore your pitch range ...

Try the same exercise while articulating and extending the following speech sounds:

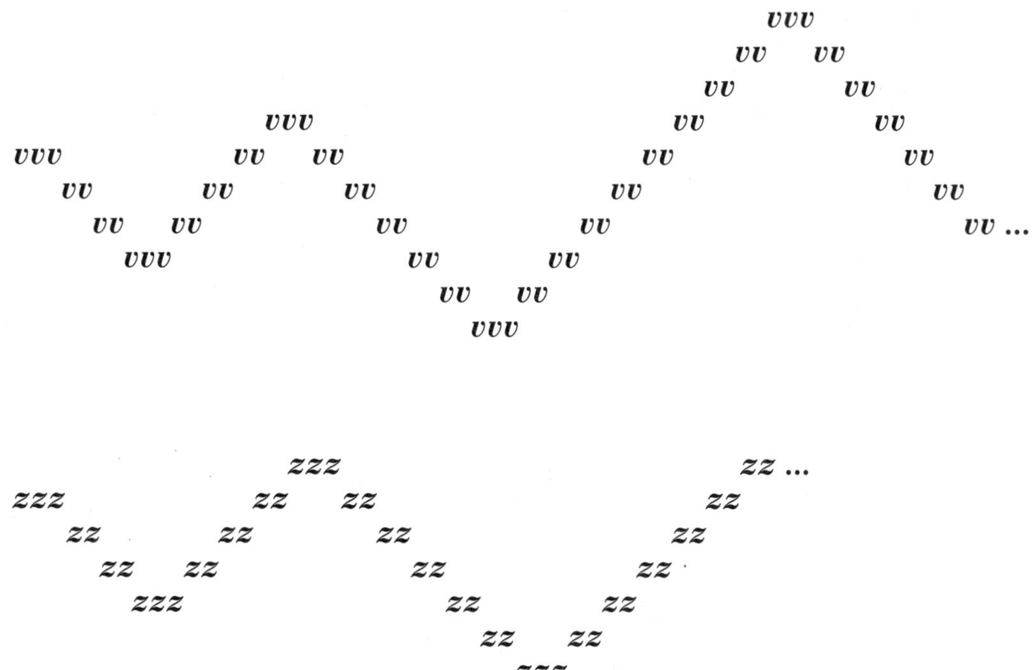

The Vocal Siren:

Now you are ready to turn your voice into a siren. You may have engaged in this type of vocal play previously without realizing you were doing a nice thing for your voice. The vowel "OO" makes an authentic siren sound, so we'll start by buzzing on "OO":

With your jaw dropped in its rest position (as always!), place your lips in the "OO" position. Starting with CVO, ignite and fuel a light "OO" into your face resonators and extend it, so you feel the buzz. Start half-way up your pitch range so you have room to expand in both directions:

"hOO!(RR) hOO-OO-OO-OO-OO-OO-OO-OO-OO..."

(let the tone be buzzy and piercing like a real siren!)

Now let the siren move around your vocal range, starting with a gradual downward slide, then sirening up and down again in ever-increasing sweeps. If you are very gentle and playful, the vocal siren will help you discover your high range without strain:

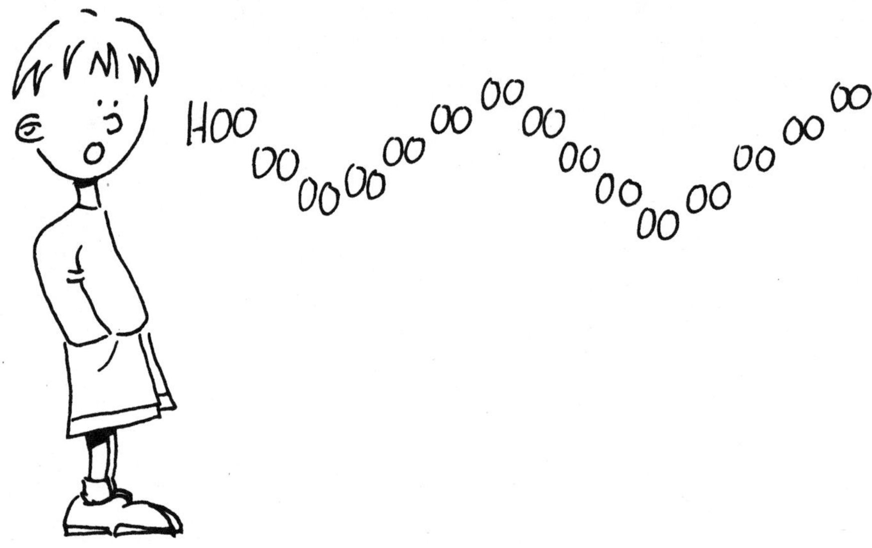

Try the vocal siren on some other sounds now. Keep the tone light but buzzy and piercing like a real siren:

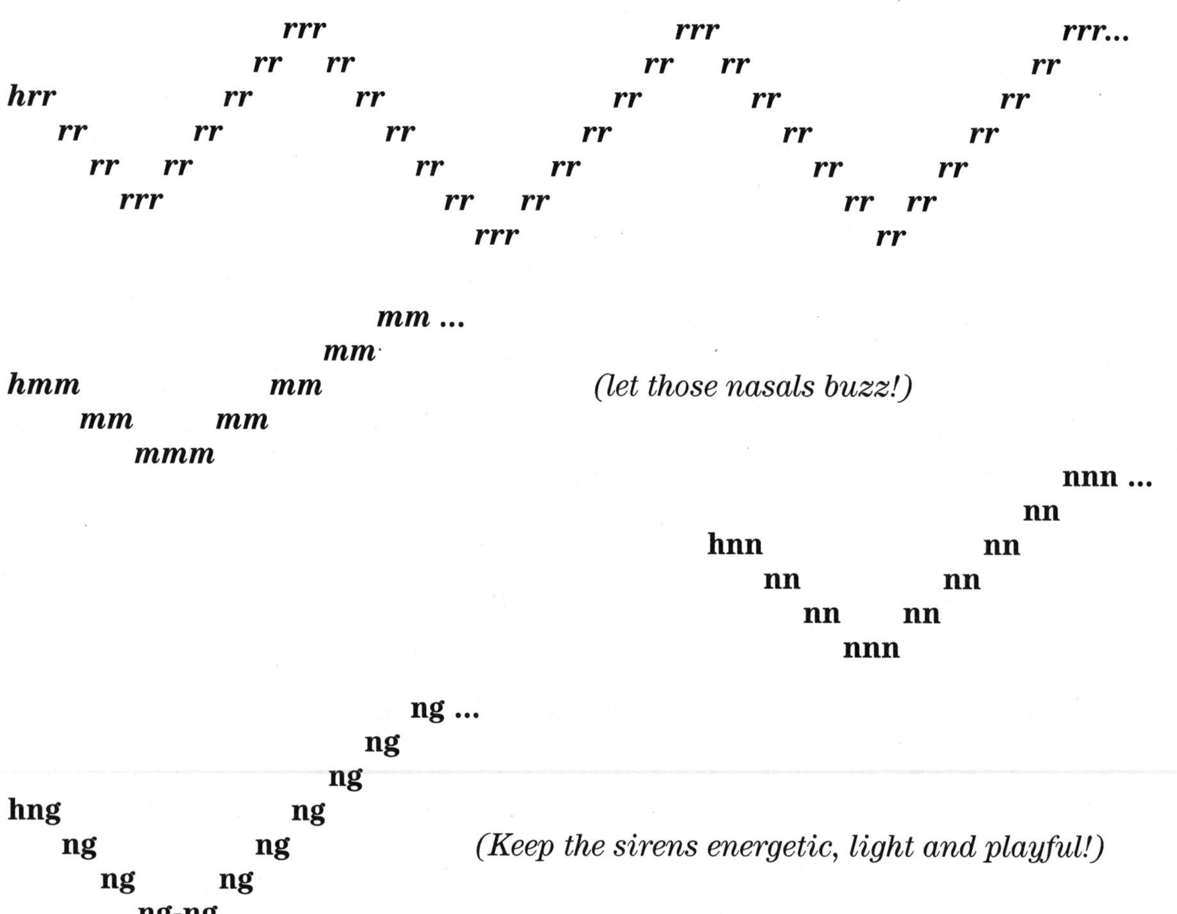

Now Let's Inflect!:

Speaking with natural pitch inflection requires a free and energetic vocal system that is responsive to, and conveys the true meaning and emotional intent of your message. Inflected speech is rewarding in several ways:

1. it energizes you and helps you connect your abdominal airflow activator to your vocal siren;

2. it prevents your voice from getting locked into a low pitch that pops and crackles and makes you want to clear your throat;

3. and it keeps your listeners alert.

A. EXPLORE AND DISCOVER:

A tape-recorder will come in very handy for the exploratory portion of your speech inflection program. You should record yourself in a variety of speaking situations to get a candid sample of your habitual speaking pitch patterns.

For each situation you have recorded, analyze your speech pattern. Describe your voice:

Is it naturally lively and variable in its pitch inflections?

or:

Is your voice a monotone monodrone?

If your speech is flat and boring, does it reflect how you were feeling about the particular situation or topic of discussion?

If it was necessary for you to talk in that situation (for example, you were doing your job) did your monodrone enhance or detract from your goals?

(for example: Did the flat voice help you dismiss an annoying customer?

or:

Would the customer have bought more if your voice had been lively, resulting in a greater commission on you part?)

Sometimes in our jobs and other aspects of life, lively inflection patterns may not reflect how we really truly feel about the situation ... however, using more pitch inflection can make us feel more energetic and interactive, and help us achieve our goals, especially if they depend on talking. In those situations, we may have to "play the role" that the situation demands, and "put on a happy voice" to get the job done well. This will require some rehearsing...

You will find your language dictates the appropriate inflection patterns if you concentrate on the meaning of your words.

Let's play with some inflections, and reflect on their effect. Keeping your voice light and lively, allow the pitch inflection on single words to rise, fall, or both. Think of the vocal siren to keep your pitch changes smooth and free. Record your productions so you can review them to confirm your voice was inflected, and to hear the effect on your message:

Well: question: *Well?*

acknowledgement/exclamation: *Well!*

dramatic response: *Well!*

Oh: question/doubt: *Oh?*

acknowledgement: *Oh.*

surprise: *Oh!*

Try enhancing your vocal inflections with a visual or physical image. Draw the pitch changes on a piece of paper as you vocalize, or sweep your hand up and down in the direction of your inflection.

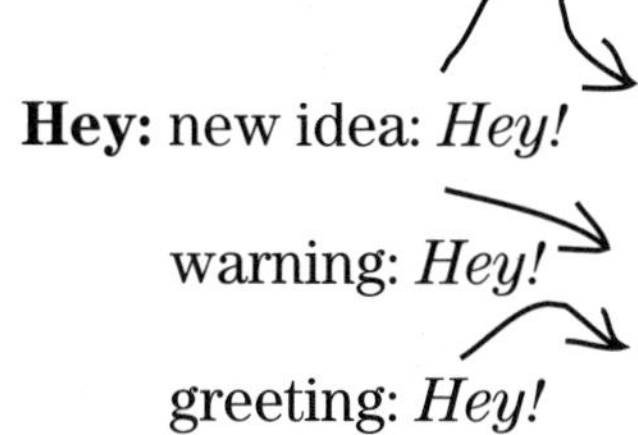
Hey: new idea: *Hey!*

warning: *Hey!*

greeting: *Hey!*

Now: command: Now!

question: *Now?*

Now try some phrases: First, draw your own arrows in above each phrase, to indicate inflections you would like to express. Use hand sweeps to enhance inflections.

Oh my!

Stop that, please!

Please help me!

Try it on.

Try it on?

Save one for me.

Can I help you?

I'll do it later.

Now, think of some phrases you use often, and practice effective inflection as you say them. Record yourself so you can confirm the effect. The longer the phrase; the more inflection "ups" and "downs" you will need. If you are accustomed to speaking in a mon-odrone, speaking with inflection may feel a bit unnatural at first. Hang in there, and listen to the positive results!

B. RE-PROGRAM THE SYSTEM:

As with Posture, CVOs, Jaw-Wag, Buzzing and all the other areas of physical reform, re-programming your speech equipment to function with natural inflection requires frequent rehearsals. By now, you are quite familiar with the rules of re-programming.

C. HABITUALIZE:

If you are rehearsing diligently to increase your dynamic pitch range and inflections, you will become familiar and comfortable with emotionally-responsive inflections during speech. You will find speech with dynamic pitch energizes you, and also captivates your communication partners and audiences.

Physical Program Step 6:

Coordinating Your Thoughts and Actions: Phrasing

A phrase is a set of words that fit together to represent a thought unit. During "physical phrasing", all words within a thought unit are linked by the flow of your voice. Ideally, the completion of a speech phrase is punctuated by a pause or full stop. Physically this means your voice flows through each phrase on the outward-bound breath, followed by a pause and RR (that is, relaxation of abdominal muscles for breath replacement).

> You will require the full cooperation of the Commander-in-Chief, the Brain, to coordinate your thoughts and language with the actions of the speech equipment.

By organizing your thoughts, planning your phrases, and "punctuating" speech with RR, you will create time to take command over the message you relay: this in turn will result in more coherent presentations and reduce the need to repeat yourself.

A. EXPLORE AND DISCOVER:

Each speech phrase is like an extended CVO of corresponding length:

Hi there! (RR) Nice day! (RR) Did you walk to work today? (RR)

hmmmm (RR) hmmmm (RR) hmmmmmmmmmmmmmmm (RR)

huuuuuh (RR) huuuuuh (RR) huuuuuuuuuuuuuuuuuuuuh (RR)

The abdominal activator sustains the vocal energy throughout each phrase, regardless of the phrase length. Of course, if you are afflicted with "motor-mouth" behaviour, you may find you run out of fuel long before your speech stops. This will cause you to strain your throat, and engage in some unnatural breathing behaviours.

Let's experiment with motor-mouth behaviour so you can recognize the affliction. Try recording it to listen to the effect of non-stop speech on your meaning. Don't punctuate or stop for breath (Speak quickly so you can get through it all on one breath!):

Say: **"Hi there nice day did you walk to work today I took the bus because I was late and I couldn't find my walking shoes anyway I'm afraid my new puppy may have chewed them yesterday when I was out shopping for groceries I needed to buy some bread so I could make my lunch today..."**

Now, that sounds (and feels) pretty silly, doesn't it!?

Let's go back a step and explore the natural way to phrase, to allow your speech equipment to perform optimally, and to give your communication partners time to absorb what you are saying:

First, review CVO:

hm!(RR) hm!(RR) hmmmmmmmmmmm(RR) hmmmmmmmmmmmm(RR)

huh!(RR) huh!(RR) huuuuuuuuuh(RR) huuuuuuuuuuuuuuuuuuuuh(RR)

Now, imagine each extended CVO is a phrase of that length. Think of some phrases you said recently, and "plot" them mentally into your CVO.

Examples:

you say:
huuuuuuuuuuuuuh(RR)

you think:
How are you Brad?

you say:
huuuuuuuuuuuuuuuuh(RR)

you think:
I hear you were sick!

Computer-Talk:

If your computer is your audience for much of your speaking day, you probably find yourself phrasing word-by-word so it can recognize your speech. This sort of phrasing is unnatural to say the least, and can cause you to strain your voice by "attacking" words with your throat valve rather than using CVO. With perseverance, you can apply CVO and an "open throat channel" to your computer talk to eliminate vocal strain.

When you are dependent on a computerized speech-recognition system, you may need to think of each *word* as a phrase. Pace yourself, so you can treat each word as a CVO, followed by RR. Remember to keep your throat channel open:

> **"I am dictating this letter to Bill**
> *hm(RR)hm(RR)hmmmm(RR)hmm(RR)hmmm(RR)hm(RR)hmm(RR)*
>
> **Mann of SomeCity, British Columbia."**
> *hmm(RR)hm(RR)hmmmmm(RR)hmmm(RR)hmmmmm.*
>
> **"Please forward a copy to his**
> *hmmm(RR)hmmmm(RR)hm(RR)hmm(RR)hm(RR)hm(RR)*
>
> **attorney in the law offices of ..."**
> *hmmmm(RR)hm(RR)hm(RR)hm(RR)hmmm(RR)hm (RR)*

"DO THEY EVER?"

B. RE-PROGRAM THE SYSTEM:

As with all other areas of physical reform, re-programming your speech equipment to phrase effectively requires frequent rehearsals. By now, you are very familiar with the principles of re-programming.

C. HABITUALIZE:

It is helpful to practice phrasing out loud, using printed text and punctuation to help you decide how to create physical phrases. Stop for RR at each obvious punctuation like:

, . : ; !

To habitualize physical phrasing in speech, first choose a passage you have memorized, like a poem, and use the natural rhythm to help you create physical phrases. Next, choose a more spontaneous speech with a format that has lots of redundancy. For example, you could describe a simple step-by-step procedure that is very familiar to you (making tea biscuits; changing a tire):

First you open your trunk, / and find your spare tire. / Next ...

Now write down monologues on some topics that are more complex. Follow grammatical punctuation rules. Highlight phrase boundaries you would like to use with /. Practice your monologues out loud, making sure you stop for RR at phrase boundaries. Let your vowels form a resonance river within phrases.

If you are rehearsing diligently to organize your thoughts and physical phrasing, it will become natural, and you will **vocalize with ease!**

This ends the physical program instruction sessions. You may use the practice charts in the appendix to guide your frequent rehearsals, or you can extract the most effective self-instructions from each section of your physical program to create a customized warm-up routine. Good Luck!

APPENDIX:

PRACTICE POSTERS

You can remove the practice posters and post them on your walls to help you conduct regular, complete and consistent vocal warm-up sessions.

Alignment and Relaxation

Release Head From Neck
"Helium-Head"

Gently Shake *"NO"*

Nod *"YES"*

Let Spine Lengthen
UNFREEZE* YOUR *KNEES!

Do the "V" Thing:

Wobble Head-Ball on Neck-Post:
BACKWARD ... FORWARD ... LEFT ... RIGHT
(note gravity as head-weight transfers)

Head Floating Upward

Posture Break

Drop Head Forward on Chest

Release Shoulders and Arms

Pivot Forward at Hip Joints

Unfreeze* Your *Knees!

Hang Out from the Hips
(if you dare)

Release Your Back and Neck:
Lengthen and Widen

Let the Breath Move the Back

Rebuild Spine Slowly: Start at the Base

Head-Ball Rolls up Last

Head Floating Upward; Spine Lengthening

Shoulders, Back, Chest Widening

DRINK SOME WATER!

Coordinated Voice Onset

Observe Breathing Cycle:
tide in ... tide out

Hold Tide Out Briefly with CVO Muscles

Release Abdomen ... *(tide rushes in)*

at Tide Out, Say: "hm!" Release Abdomen ...
(tide rushes in)

Repeat CVO(RR) CVO(RR) ...: hm!(RR) hm!(RR) ...

(keep the actions flexible and playful!)

Drop Jaw and Tongue

at Tide Out, Say: "huh!" Release Abdomen ...
(tide rushes in)

Repeat CVO(RR) CVO(RR) ...: huh!(RR) huh!(RR) ...

HAVE A SIP OF WATER!

Extend CVO and Get the Buzz

Helium-Head OR "Hanging Out";
Extend CVO Followed by RR:

hm!(RR)hmmmmmmmmmmm(RR)

(indulge the buzz in the resonators)

Let the Buzz Travel and Expand:

hm!(RR)hmmmmmmmmmmm...(RR)

(feel it with your hands and sensors!)

BUZZ: hn!(RR)hnnnnnnnnnnnn...(RR)

BUZZ: hng!(RR)hngngngngng...(RR)

Let the Buzz Travel and Slide:

hmm m mm m m m mmm m m m m m mm m m

Aerobicise Your Face

Do these face-ups repeatedly:

RAISE AND LOWER EYEBROWS

OPEN EYES WIDE; SQUEEZE SHUT

RAISE AND LOWER NOSE

RAISE AND LOWER CHEEKS

PUSH LIPS FORWARD AND BACK

CLENCH AND UNCLENCH YOUR TEETH

PUSH YOUR LOWER LIP DOWN AND UP

RELAX YOUR ENTIRE FACE!

Lippy Doo-Dah:

Stretch Lips Forward and Back Vocalizing Lightly for:

oo-ee-oo-ee-oo-ee-oo-ee-oo-ee-oo-ee ...

O-ay-O-ay-O-ay-O-ay-O-ay-O-ay-O-ay ...

or-ah-or-ah-or-ah-or-ah-or-ah-or-ah ..

The Tongue Is a Rug

Breathe Through your Mouth
Hang Out the Rug

Slowly Release
Tongue-Rug
Forward Out and
Down

(monitor TJ muscles under the chin)

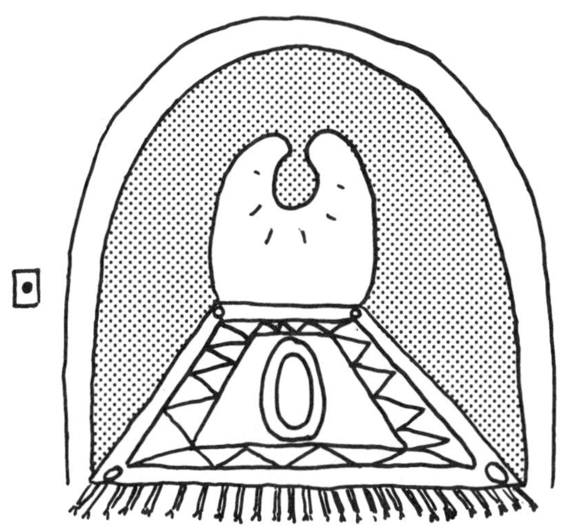

Rug Roll:

Let a Smooth Tone Come Out over the Roll:

HuhYuhYuhYuhYuhYuhYuhYuhYuh...

Monitor TJ Muscles Under your Chin

Extend a CVO from Mouth-Open Position:

huh!(RR) huuuuuuuuuuuuuuu...(RR)
(tongue and TJ muscles stay passive)

The Jaw of Gravity

Clench and Unclench Teeth

Let your Jaw Drop Open

Tip Head-Weight Back Slightly:

Jaw Hanging Off the Face

Push it Closed with your Hand, Release

Repeat Hand-Closed Jaw ... Jaw Drop

Pivot Jaw Up and Down with your Hand
(no bulging on sides of face!)

Be a Marionette from Mars:

Jaw Drops for Each Vowel ***(the tongue is a rug):***

AnAnAnAnAnAnAnAnAnAnAnAnAnAnA..
↓ ↓ ↓ ↓ ↓ ↓ ↓ ↓ ↓ ↓ ↓ ↓ ↓ ↓ ↓

AsAsAsAsA...; AYdAYdAYdAY...; OnOnOnOnO...
↓ ↓ ↓ ↓ ↓ ↓ ↓ ↓ ↓ ↓ ↓ ↓ ↓ ↓

AnAnAnOne,Two,Three,Four,Five...
↓ ↓ ↓ ↓ ↓ ↓ ↓ ↓

HAVE A DRINK OF WATER!

Get the Buzz on Speech

Hum-Buzz with CVO:

MMMake the MMMost of Hummmm-Dingers:

Mmmmakmmmormmmonnnnneee ***(make more money)***

Nninnmmorlongngmmils ***(nine more long miles)***

Nnow you mmake up somme mmore humm-dingers!

Vowel-Buzz with CVO:

huh!(RR) huuuuuuuuuuuuuuuuuuuuuuuuuuuuuh...

hOOOOOOOOOOOOOOOOOOOOOOOOOOOO ...

hOO-OO-OO-OO-OO-OO-OO-OO-OO ...

hEE-EE-EE-EE-EE-EE-EE-EE-EE ...

hAY-AY-AY-AY-AY-AY-AY-AY-AY ...

Review and Do Jaw-Wag, Lippy Speech to Let the Vowels Buzz Inside and Ring Outside!

Pitch 'n Play

Use the Lip-Bubble or Tongue Trill to Play with Pitch
(keep the tones light but clear):

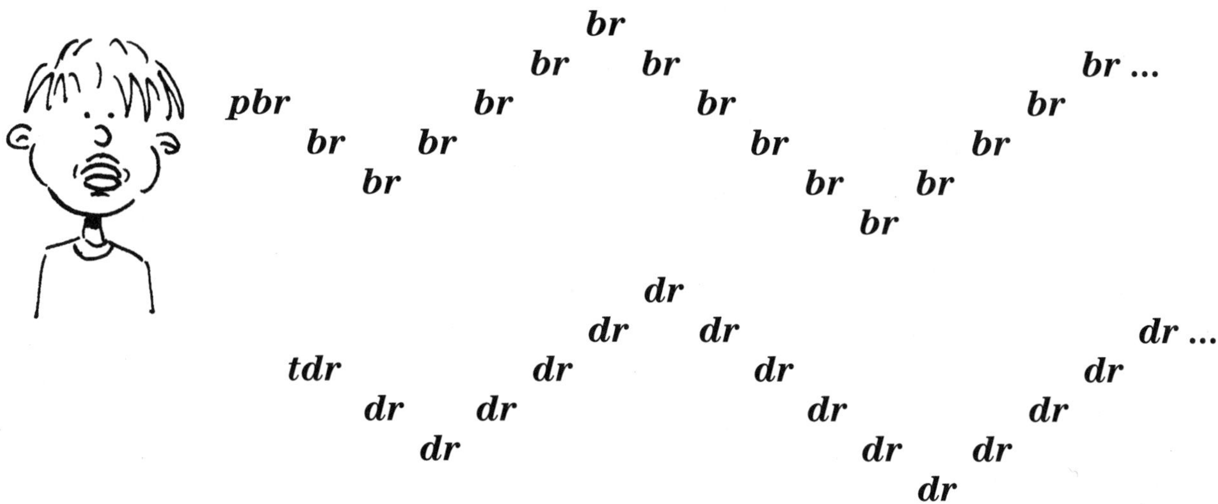

Use the Finger Kazoo and Other Buzzy Sounds to Play with Pitch: *(keep the tones light):*

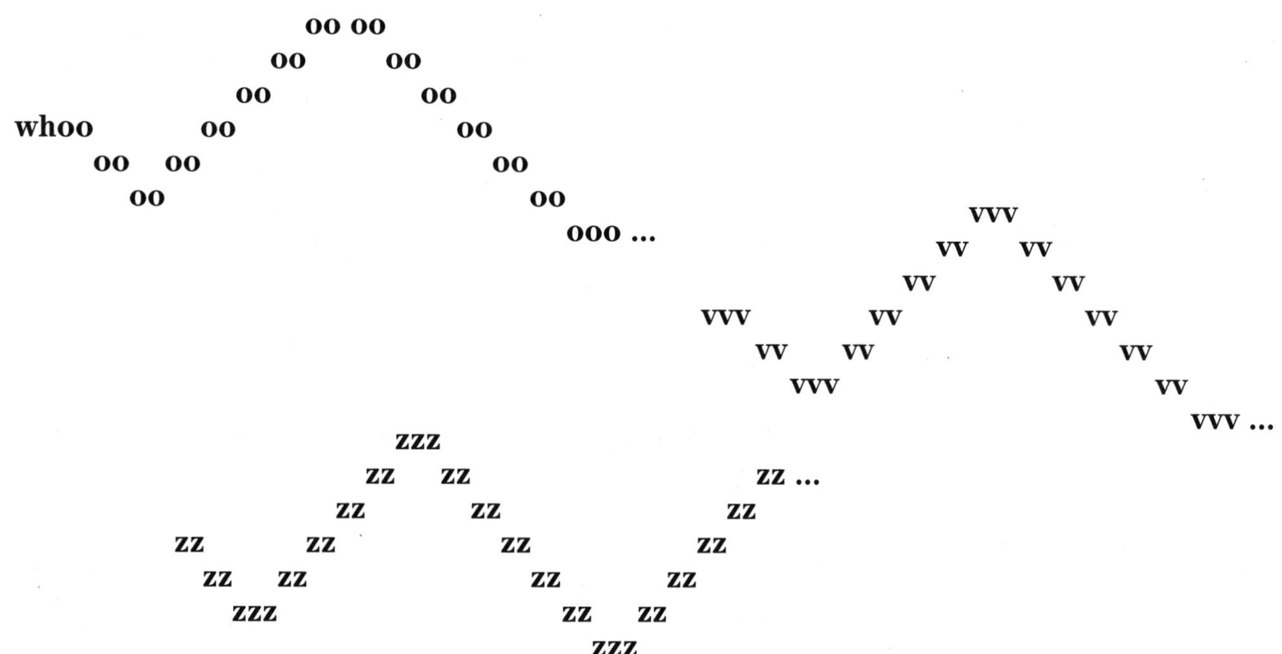

Sirens Away

Add some Meaningful Inflection to Your Speech with the Light Playful Siren Effect:

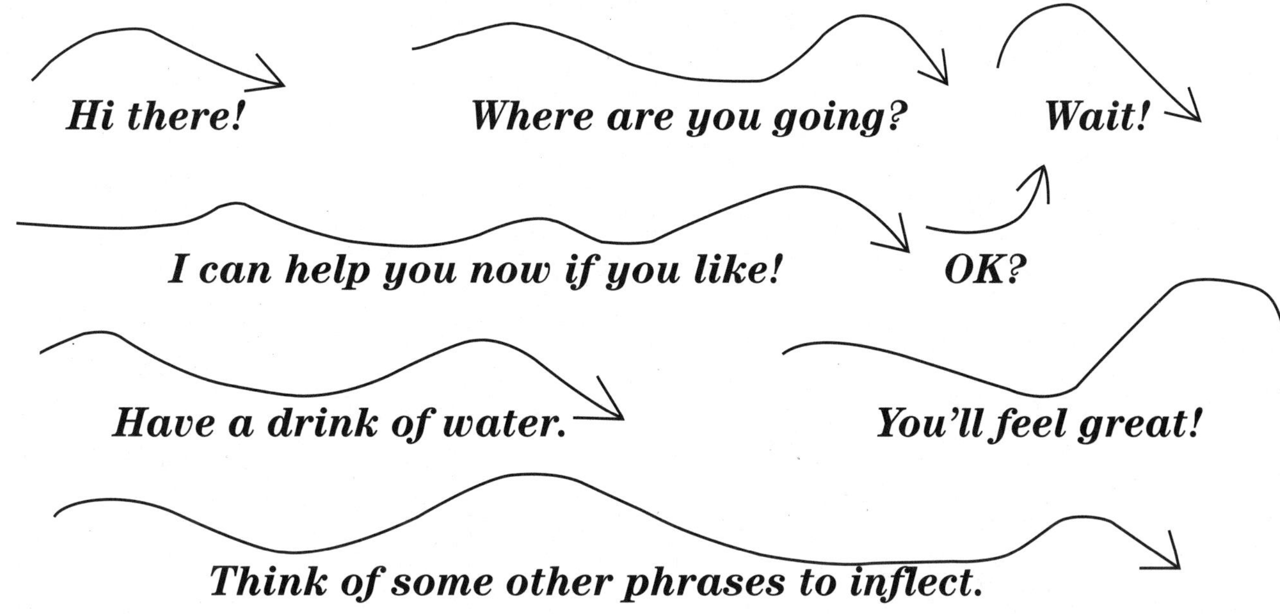

Speaking of Phrases(RR)!

Starting with CVO, Generate Imaginary Phrases of Different Lengths:

hm!(RR) hmmmm(RR) hmmmmmmmmmmmm(RR)

huh!(RR) huuuuuuuuuuh(RR) huuuuuuuuuuuuh(RR)

(imagine some real phrases into the CVOs)

Try some Short Phrases with Speech, Keeping CVO(RR) in Mind and Body. The Vocal Tone Flows Through the Vowels within a Phrase:

Hi there (RR) How've you been? (RR) Maybe we should stop (RR)

so we can catch our breath (RR) and relax for a minute (RR)

Don't you think that would be a good idea? (RR)

Try some more phrases now (RR) ...

Mark some text for logical phrasing (RR) Then read it aloud to apply physical phrases (RR) and to Vocalize with Ease!(RR) Practice phrasing your speeches,(RR) lectures,(RR) Debates,(RR) etc. ...

About the Author:

Linda Rammage is a speech-language pathologist who specializes in disorders of voice. Dr. Rammage's work has evolved from many years of studying and practising the science and art of vocalizing (as a talker, a clinician, a teacher, a researcher, a dog-mom*, and an amateur singer). This self-improvement guide is a collection of therapy techniques Dr. Rammage has been using successfully with her clients for over fifteen years.

Dr. Rammage is also co-author of a well-known professional textbook entitled "The Management of Voice Disorders" (Morrison & Rammage, copyright 1994. Chapman & Hall Medical ISBN: 0-412-35090-4; Singular Publishing Group ISBN: 1-56593-311-7)

*Hank and Benny

About the Illustrator:

Michiel Haijtink is a freelance artist, illustrator, cartoonist and painter living in Vancouver. Originally from the Netherlands, Michiel immigrated to Canada in 1994.

BIBLIOGRAPHY:

Barlow, Wilfred. 1973. *The Alexander Technique.* New York: Warner Books.

Lessac, Arthur. 1967. *The Use and Training of the Human Voice.* (2nd edition) New York: Drama Book Publishers.

Linklater, Kristin. 1976. *Freeing the Natural Voice.* New York: Drama Book Publishers.

Morrison, Murray; Rammage, Linda; Nichol, Hamish; Pullan, Bruce; May, Phillip; Salkeld, Lesley. 1994. *The Management of Voice Disorders.* London: Chapman & Hall Medical; San Diego: Singular Publishing Group Inc.

ORDER FORMS:

For additional copies of this self-improvement guide, please send this order sheet, along with your money order or certified cheque payable to:

VOCALIZING WITH EASE
c/o Pacific Voice Clinic
805 West 12th Ave
Vancouver, B.C.
V5Z 1M9

Price per copy: $35.00
Bulk orders (20 copies or more) Price per copy: $30.00

Mail____________copies of Vocalizing with Ease to:

Name:____Company: ______________________

Address: ____

____Postal Code: ____________________

Amount Enclosed: $

****

For additional copies of this self-improvement guide, please send this order sheet, along with your money order or certified cheque payable to:

VOCALIZING WITH EASE
c/o Pacific Voice Clinic
805 West 12th Ave
Vancouver, B.C.
V5Z 1M9

Price per copy: $35.00
Bulk orders (20 copies or more) Price per copy: $30.00

Mail____________copies of Vocalizing with Ease to:

Name:____Company: ______________________

Address: ____

____Postal Code: ____________________

Amount Enclosed: $